Arbitrary Order: Paintings by **Pat Steir**

Contemporary Arts Museum
Houston, Texas

May 27 — July 17, 1983

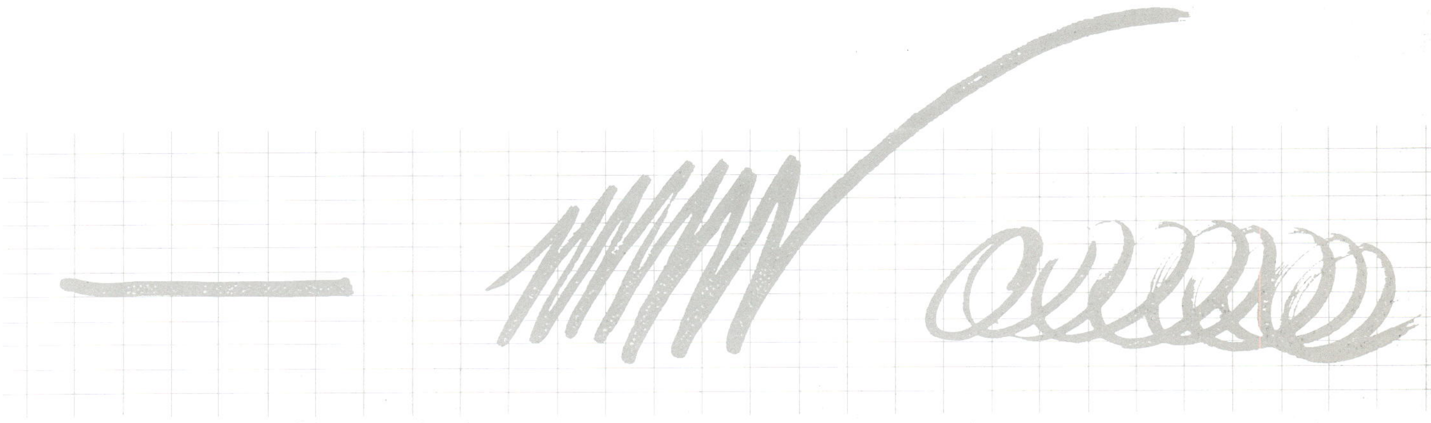

Arbitrary Order: Paintings by Pat Steir has been supported by a grant from CHASE MANHATTAN of TEXAS with additional support from Mrs. Hyman Finger.

The catalogue, *Arbitrary Order: Paintings by Pat Steir*, has been funded through the **Contemporary Arts Publication Fund** established by The Charles Engelhard Foundation in May 1982 with additional support from The Brown Foundation, Inc., Houston, Texas.

Exhibition and catalogue prepared by Marti Mayo
with the assistance of Emily L. Todd
Contemporary Arts Museum, Houston
May 27–July 17, 1983

The graphic marks appearing throughout this catalogue were executed by Pat Steir especially for this publication.

Library of Congress Card Catalogue Number 83-70897
ISBN 0-936080-10-8
This publication has been prepared in conjunction with the exhibition *Arbitrary Order: Paintings by Pat Steir*, organized by Marti Mayo for the **Contemporary Arts Museum**, Houston, Texas. May 27–July 17, 1983

Lenders to the **Exhibition**

Mr. and Mrs. Anthony J. A. Bryan
Mr. and Mrs. Armand J. Castellani
Mr. and Mrs. Victor W. Ganz
Richard M. Hollander, Kansas City, Missouri
Sydney and Frances Lewis
Sol LeWitt
Vera Q. List
Gloria and Leonard Luria
Martin Melzer
Mr. and Mrs. S. I. Newhouse, Jr.
Mr. and Mrs. Laughlin Phillips
Steven D. Robinson
Pat Steir

Albright-Knox Art Gallery
The Art Museum, Princeton University
The Chase Manhattan Bank
Dallas Museum of Fine Arts
Ponderosa Inc., Dayton, Ohio
The Prudential Insurance Company of America
Wadsworth Atheneum
Whitney Museum of American Art, New York

Eason Gallery, Santa Fe, New Mexico
McIntosh/Drysdale Gallery, Houston, Texas
Max Protetch Gallery, New York, New York

Cover:
Chrysanthemum 1981
Oil on canvas
3 panels, each 60 × 60
Collection Gloria and Leonard Luria

Table of Contents

2 **Lenders to the Exhibition**

4 **Foreword**
Linda L. Cathcart

5 **Acknowledgments**
Marti Mayo

6 **Arbitrary Order: Paintings by Pat Steir**
Marti Mayo

16 **Conversation with Pat Steir**
Ted Castle

23 **Catalogue of the Exhibition**

25 **Color Plates**

33 **Black and White Plates**

47 **Pat Steir: Chronology, Exhibitions, Bibliography**
Emily L. Todd

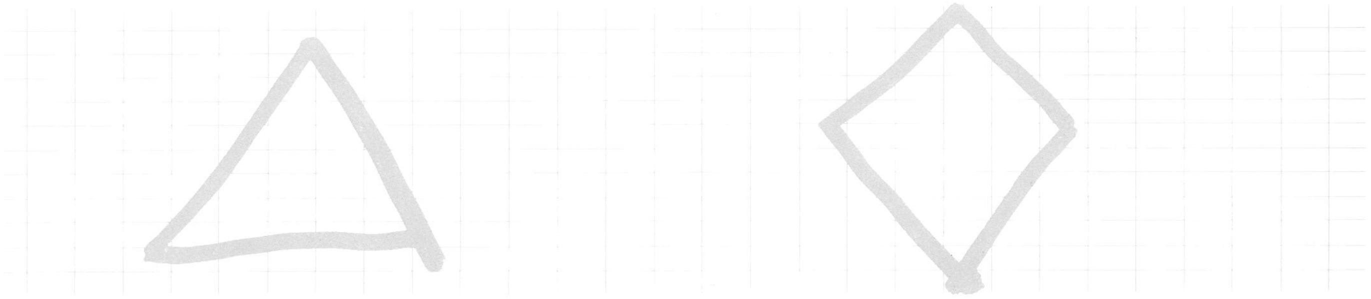

Foreword

It is a great pleasure for the Contemporary Arts Museum to present the first large-scale exhibition of paintings by New York artist Pat Steir. We are fortunate to be able to mount this exhibition in conjunction with the presentation of an exhibition of Steir's graphic work, organized by Dr. Elizabeth Broun, Curator of Prints and Drawings and Acting Director at the Spencer Museum of Art, The University of Kansas, Lawrence. Seen concurrently, *Form Illusion Myth: Prints and Drawings of Pat Steir* and *Arbitrary Order: Paintings by Pat Steir* will allow Houstonians a rare chance to see a large amount of the artist's work at one time and to assess the relationships and differences in her work in diverse media. Although Steir has exhibited widely in this country and in Europe during the last decade, her mature work has never before been assembled for comprehensive viewing. These two exhibitions will allow a full opportunity to view the evolution of the artist's work as well as to better evaluate and understand her contributions to the vocabulary of this decade.

Since 1979, major exhibitions organized or exhibited by the Contemporary Arts Museum have been devoted either to mid-career surveys of the work of major figures in contemporary art or to thematic group exhibitions of work by artists of this region and other parts of the country. *Arbitrary Order: Paintings by Pat Steir* admirably suits the first catagory and is presented in a tradition of exhibitions organized by the Contemporary Arts Museum, as well as by other institutions, of the work of Ansel Adams, Richard Artschwager, John Baldessari, Roger Brown, Robert Gordy, Nancy Graves, Robert Morris, Ree Morton and others.

The Houston presentation of *Form Illusion Myth: Prints and Drawings of Pat Steir* is partially funded through a joint grant from the Texas Commission on the Arts and the National Endowment for the Arts. On behalf of myself and the Board of Trustees I would like to acknowledge the generous financial support provided to *Arbitrary Order: Paintings by Pat Steir* by Chase Manhattan of Texas and by Museum patron, Mrs. Hyman Finger. Publication of this catalogue has been made possible by a special fund — the **Contemporary Arts Publication Fund** established by The Charles Engelhard Foundation in May 1982 and now supported with additional funds from The Brown Foundation, Inc., Houston, Texas. The generosity and foresight of these corporations, foundations and individuals have made it possible for the Contemporary Arts Museum to contribute to the documentation of the contemporary arts in a serious and considered way. We are very grateful for their contributions.

It gives me special pleasure to acknowledge Curator Marti Mayo and the others on our staff who shared the tasks of organizing this exhibition with her. Finally, it has been a great privilege for me to have known Pat Steir for many years and to have been able to see her work evolve. She is an artist who deserves our closest attention.

Linda L. Cathcart
Director

Acknowledgments

Each exhibition, whether large or small, makes its own demands on the institution and its staff. These demands vary in intensity and in nature. But, in every case, the exhibition's curator is indebted to those dedicated and professional people who help the project progress from a proposal on paper to the actual presentation of the art and publication of the catalogue. *Arbitrary Order: Paintings by Pat Steir* is no exception, and I would like to thank those who have given freely of their time and energy for this project.

As always, Director Linda L. Cathcart has rendered the most special and valuable aid. Her continuing commitment to excellence and her support of the curatorial staff is unwavering and much appreciated. Emily L. Todd, curatorial assistant, has helped with every aspect of the exhibition and publication and has prepared the documentation on the artist for the catalogue. Timothy Walters, public relations and publications officer, has lent his support and encouragement, editing and coordinating the publication of the catalogue. Lynn Hurst, curatorial secretary, has worked many hours typing the manuscript, and Michael Barry, head preparator and Clay Henley, assistant preparator, have installed the exhibition with their usual unusual competence and skill. Registrar Emily Croll has ably overseen the loans and their transportation.

A very special thanks is due to the lenders. Lenders are, in fact, a major part of the success of this institution. Because the Contemporary Arts Museum has no permanent collection, all exhibited works of art are borrowed from individual and institutional lenders. The trust of the lenders and their continued generosity make our exhibition program possible. I gratefully acknowledge the invaluable contribution of the lenders to this exhibition; by parting with their works of art for a time, they have made it possible for us and our audience to enjoy them, thereby enriching our experience of art.

I also wish to acknowledge Dr. Elizabeth Broun, Curator of Prints and Drawings and Acting Director, the Spencer Museum of Art, The University of Kansas, Lawrence, for her counsel and concerned cooperation. Dr. Broun and I each independently conceived of organizing an exhibition of Steir's work around the same time. She wished to concentrate on the prints and drawings for the Spencer while I was interested in organizing a show of the paintings. I am most pleased we will be able to mount both shows here in Houston. Broun's *Form Illusion Myth: Prints and Drawings of Pat Steir* is an invaluable compliment to the *Arbitrary Order* show, allowing the Houston audience a complete overview of the work of this important artist.

Max Protetch of the Max Protetch Gallery, New York, New York, rendered valuable aid in the beginning stages of the project and during its evolution. Michael R. Klein, formerly director of the Gallery and presently a free-lance curator who acts as an agent for Pat Steir, has been helpful in solving innumerable problems, including locating works; and for his assistance and support, through every step of the organization of the exhibition and catalogue, I am deeply grateful. Ted Castle, a New York writer, has contributed a valuable interview with the artist to this publication.

Finally, I would like to thank the artist. Over the past two years, she has been actively involved in the entire project and has been generous with her time and energy. Her cooperation has been invaluable.

Marti Mayo
Curator

Arbitrary Order: Paintings by **Pat Steir**

I'm not interested in meaning in a daily way. I'm interested in the way scientists deal with it, in a kind of fake order. I'm interested in many different kinds of arbitrary order. Starting with a mark and bringing it to a figure is one of the kinds of arbitrary order, discovering the fact that figurative and abstract art are the same thing . . . . Abstraction and figuration are different ways to inspect the same thing — an image and its meaning, or a mark and how it can seem to become an image when it's really just a mark.

Pat Steir, 1982[1]

One day in 1971, Pat Steir — who was then an emerging New York artist of some reputation — made a strange painting that came to be called *Bird*. The painting, as Steir herself and others have recounted, was at least superficially the result of the gift of a bird from a close friend. Another friend made it a cage and Steir named the bird John Cage — for obvious reasons and also out of admiration for that now near legendary avant-garde artist and musician. This painting deeply disturbed Steir. At the time, she didn't understand where it had come from in terms of her preceding work or what it meant. She wasn't even sure it was a painting. She says, "I called a friend in and I said, 'Ah, look at that. Do you think that's a painting?' It broke away from what my standard idea of a painting was."[2] Looking back, Steir now considers *Bird* to be the first of more than 100 paintings, made in loosely defined series, that would address ideas and concepts about how we think, how we perceive and how we construct systems of information which allow us to communicate with others, both visually and verbally.

Along the way in her research — Steir sees both her art and poetry as research — she would question meaning in personal expression, the use of signs and symbols, issues in art, art history and art criticism and the very act of painting itself. She would make paintings which appear diverse in formal intention, but which have recurrent images used in a variety of ways, and which all have in common the fact that they are visual representations of her ideas. All Steir's art is intensely personal, in that it is a direct (if not always clear) reflection of herself and her thinking as well as of the idea she is interested in explaining to herself and the viewer. Often, her work appears totally out of step with the mainstream of painting at the time, but just as often it appears to coincide with it. These departures from and crossing paths with ideas and forms found in the work of other artists working in more defined parameters are almost like accidental intersections of paths leading in different directions. And Steir's path has always been a private one which meandered through the most interesting of territories — some explored in concert with other artists and some quite alone. That path is the subject of this discussion.

Pat Steir was born in Newark, New Jersey, in 1940, the eldest of four children. Early in her childhood, she was recognized as gifted, and as she grew up she exhibited aspects of her gifts both in art and in poetry. Her father encouraged her to pursue a literary career, but Steir chose to enroll in 1956 at Pratt Institute in New York City to study art. There, she was influenced by the painter Richard Lindner. Steir credits Lindner with encouraging her to work within her own individual vision and direction rather than to experiment with the ideas and techniques that were then "in the air." In a recent interview, Steir said,

> Most of the teachers and the influences were abstract expressionist. I painted with a #1 brush — a #1 sable brush . . . . I had an idea and I stuck to it. When I didn't . . . Lindner yelled at me for being so easily influenced . . . In a way, I didn't think I could paint [in an abstract expressionist manner] until very recently, when I discovered I could. It always seemed too athletic.[3]

Lindner, a realist painter whose work is also difficult to identify with a single style or movement, was both a visual and an intellectual influence on Steir, and her early paintings relate to his in their use of a compressed space and graphic distortion of the figure. These early works of Steir contained images of people, animals or things, but they soon contained figures either running through splashes of paint, surrounded by storms of paint or set in very expressionistically rendered landscapes.[4] These splashes and landscapes were Steir's reaction to abstract expressionism and its emphasis on both process — the act of painting — and the resulting artist's mark. This interest in the act and the mark are her heritage from the New York School; from Lindner she acquired a confidence in the pursuit of her own vision.

After attending Pratt for two years, Steir moved to Cambridge, Massachusetts, and studied philosophy and literature at Boston University. It was there that she became acquainted with the work of Gottfried Wilhelm von Leibnitz (1646-1716), a mathematician and philosopher who invented many of the mathematical signs we still use. Her discovery of his work coincided with an interest of Steir's which would become increasingly important in her paintings — the meaning of signs and symbols and their origins as well as their relationship to the things they represent.

Pat Steir returned to New York and to Pratt and completed her B.F.A. in 1961. She had her first one-person show in 1964 and continued to show sporadically throughout the decade. The paintings of the sixties — mostly lost or destroyed — evolved from the small-scale student work to much larger paintings, often measuring seven by twelve feet. The work of the late sixties, like the work done at Pratt, also contained figures, compressed space and were symmetrical and static. The figures were male nudes with animal heads; Steir calls them wolf-men. These strange paintings with their surreal juxtapositions and disciplined format reflect the influence of the work of Lindner and of Vincent Van Gogh. Van Gogh's personal expressionism and use of space to reinforce and inform the meaning of his work affected Steir's paintings. Completed at the height of minimalism and of conceptual art, these tortured and dramatic paintings are an example of the individual path Steir had embarked upon. She was a New York artist who was well-acquainted with the work of other artists and with the kinds of ideas they were involved in; yet this body of work was very much apart from the mainstream of the time. In fact, these works from the sixties look more at home in the eighties — more related to the new figuration and neo-expressionism — than to the art of that time.

When Pat Steir painted *Bird*, it had little precedent in relation to these wolf-men paintings. No closer to mainstream painting than the figures had been, this new work was full of unconnected images — a bird, the sky, swatches of paint, grid lines — marks of paint placed arbitrarily all over the canvas in distinctly separate fields. It appeared to have no logic, formal or intellectual, and Steir now realizes that *Bird* and another painting which quickly followed, *Blue*, 1971, were reactions to a confusion in her own life as well as to the chaos she saw in the world around her. In the same way as Cage had incorporated chance and chaos into his music, Steir chose (at first unconsciously) to "Put a lid over chaos; I saw that these paintings were the chaos that I felt, and that I would try to paint chaos — to picture a portion of the world, with all its illogical relationships and juxtapositions."[5] The bird became for Steir a sign not only for the figure but also for paint and for representation itself. The other pictorial elements incorporated in the painting took their meaning from similar and private ideas. *Bird* marked the beginning of a series of about fifteen paintings made during 1972 that evidence Steir's interest in order or the absence of order in physical and psychological phenomena.

Looking for the Mountain, 1971, is the earliest painting included in this exhibition and was completed after the artist visited the reclusive painter, Agnes Martin, at Martin's home in the mountains of New Mexico.[6] This trip and the visit with Martin — an individualistic woman whose minimal, delicately colored paintings containing lines and grids, and which represent but do not picture landscape — were a mythic and metaphorical experience for Steir.[7]

Bird, *Blue* and *Looking for the Mountain* were completed almost concurrently and represent the transition of her painting to the narrative, poetic and storytelling or mythlike works of 1972. They make evident Steir's concern with meaning conveyed in visual terms and her obsession with the artist's mark. In these works she would develop a lexicon of both marks and images that form the basis for a personal visual vocabulary, neither particularly expressionist nor symbolic — at least in intention — which continues to inform her work. Although this personal lexicon takes many forms and exhibits different emphases placed on certain elements, it, like language, is a system for the artist — a system which allows personal concerns to be expressed by her — the artist, the mythmaker, the storyteller.

Looking for the Mountain can be seen as both a transition from the sixties work to that of 1971 and as a step on the path to the important paintings of 1972. The painting is still very formal in composition. It has a border made of brushstrokes laying perpendicular to the canvas' edge. Slightly right of center is a large pink-orange field bisected by a broken, irregular grid which is also evident in the narrower shape set at the left. This shape set at the left appears somewhat like a geologist's bisection of part of the land and contains irregular drips where the paint has been allowed to find its own way to the bottom of the form. The painting contains five silhouettes, or partial silhouettes of mountains — much as one might see while driving in the West. A half-circle, an obviously man-made object not related to nature or feeling, peeks in at the upper right-hand corner of the large field and croplike marks surround the field. These elements may be seen as devices which remind us that this is a painting made from certain devices available to the artist — paint, shape, color. *Looking for the Mountain* relates to Steir's works of the sixties in its formal organization, but a sense of time is signaled by the grid which allows us to conceive of a progression of visual events. The grid is as well an indication or sign, for Steir, of space. The painting has become a vehicle for a narrative — albeit an obtuse and non-linear one, which is non-specific. It is as if she is painting a myth or fable rather than a novel. This work along with *Bird* and *Blue* is the first of many in which shapes and marks are placed on the surface with the kind of sensitivity to their meaning in space as a poet (which Steir is) might attach to the placement of words on the space of a page.[8]

Cellar Door, The Answer for Anita and Leibnitz, Three Green Days and *Border Lord* are representative works from 1972. All have in common an apparently unordered or chaotic appearance. Joan Simon has remarked that they even appear unfinished, as if the artist had rushed from one to explore the space and images in another.[9] Steir has said that it was difficult for her to let these works display such disorder. After all, the point of art is the making of some kind of visual order which carries meaning, but at this time she wished to convey a sense of the chaos of the universe. For though man imposes signs and systems, orders which are understandable to him, these systems exist within himself rather than in our mutable world. Like Cage, Steir was interested in reflecting this chaos by employing the device of chance or accident in her work.

Random brushmarks, X-marks, squares of primary colors, and squares of tonal gradations in browns and greys are present on the grids and fields in these paintings. The squares are similar in form to the color bars used by photographers to measure accuracy of the color when photographing an object and refer, for Steir, to the process as well as "truth." The paintings of this period each have some sort of central shape which echoes the shape of the canvas, and they are bound by formal borders painted by the artist. Drips of paint in the works all refer to the process of art-making.

In Steir's work, various images — the mountains, birds, shells, flowers and skies — also overlay the fields and grids. Her representational images are not the subconscious symbols of the surrealistic repertoire but rather signs of both specific and non-specific reference points for the artist. Marcia Tucker has written, "In her work, the pictorial and formal equivalences of our spoken and written language are so altered, so unusual and honest, that they are unequivocally resistant to the kind of generalized psycho-sexual symbolizing that is found, for example, in surrealist narration."[10]

For Steir, her marks, squares and images form a set of signs which take meaning from the thing they represent — like numbers or words. These signs signify rather than symbolize and, like words and numbers, are representative of something. Also, like words, Steir's signs take on meaning depending on their context, their order and use in relationship to one another. In these 1972 works the artist is using signs as a poet uses words, and the meaning conveyed by either may be symbolic — but these paintings are narrative in the broadest sense. They are painted "proceeding from an event to its memory, from the memory to the story of it."[11] The story each conveys is constructed of incomplete phrases from a private language which allow us to intuit meaning rather than be informed of it. As in a myth or fable, we are being shown a maxim or truth, but it may be obtuse and open to individual interpretation.[12]

These most personal paintings contain, somewhat paradoxically, a myriad of art historical references which reflect Steir's individual commentary on art and reflect her love affair with art in general and the work of specific artists in particular. The grids and color fields can be seen as referring to both conceptual and minimal art — they are common devices seen in both those very highly intellectualized ways of working. In Steir's work, grids and fields produce disorder, rather than expressing a gestalt or ordering systems of presentation, as in conceptualism or minimalism. They are also an acknowledgment of and homage to the work of Sol LeWitt and Agnes Martin — both of whom are personal friends, important to Steir's development. Her white-on-white fields are reminiscent of the work of Robert Ryman; Steir's drips and sometimes waxy-surfaces relate to those of Brice Marden.[13] While reviewing her 1972 exhibition at Paley & Lowe Gallery in New York, John Canaday commented sensitively on this aspect of her work. While he found several sources in her work, "hard-edgers, neo-dadists, popists, minimalists, sharp-focused realism and others" and said that one might call it eclectic, he concluded, "Miss Steir can no more be accused of eclecticism than a poet can be accused of plagiarizing because he has not invented his own vocabulary to express an individual sentiment. Whatever she uses, she uses in her own way for her very own personal communication with the observer."[14] Canaday compared her visual homage to language in poetry, but this use of sources might, as well, be compared to a scientist, who builds his own research on the foundations of the work of others.

In addition to the brushmarks and informalized color charts and drips which indicate the process of painting, Steir inaugurates the use of an X-mark in the works from 1972. The artist indicates her dissatisfaction with or distrust of an image or section of the painting with its use. Steir is too sophisticated an artist not to be aware that the placement of this X over an image, which is rendered representationally, reasserts the integrity of the picture plane as a two-dimensional surface, but, in this series of paintings, she uses it primarily to indicate process and to allow us to see that process and participate in its evaluation.

By 1973, Steir admits, she was exhausted with the effort to portray chaos she found in herself and in the world, and turned instead to concentrate on an issue hinted at in the 1972 paintings. She became interested in the dichotomy of a painting as an abstraction — a painting as an object — juxtaposed with the representation of the realistic image. This change in concentration resulted in a series of formidably elegant works, composed of a black field, bounded by Steir's ever-present border, whose center was dominated by the image of a flower. This complete switch in format was a direct reaction to the asymmetrical and deliberate spacial confusion in the work of 1972 and to her move to southern California. From 1973 to 1975, she taught at California Institute for the Arts, returning to New York to work at regular intervals. "I moved to sunny California," Steir says, "pulled the curtains and painted everything black. I saw everything out there in silhouette."[15] The first of these paintings *Black*, 1973, like many of the 1972 works, is a large horizontal painting. It has in common with those paintings the color bars and border, but the center iris anchors the more eccentric and disparate elements of the composition. This center flower is crossed out with an X-mark, as are the other irises in the right-hand border of the canvas. In this work, the X serves a formal rather than a symbolic purpose. But a flower crossed out with the X will become an important symbol in 1974. Other works from 1973, *Breadfruit*, *Line Lima* and *Night Chant Series, Number 3 Dawn* all are characterized by the central black field.

Line Lima, says Steir, is about the evolution of a single mark to an image — a lesson about the ideas in art, the making of art and the perceiving of art. Although its central image is not visually dominant, it is conceptually important. The center of the field contains the green, broken outline of lima beans in a group of pods. From this image various dotted lines radiate outward to a series of signs — a brushstroke, a black-and-white rendering of the image, scratchlike marks, etc. The border contains three squares — red, blue, yellow — drips and a red image of the bean pod. We are also shown the pod, fully rendered in color, and a close-up of a lima bean.

In *Breadfruit*, Steir simplifies visual elements even further. There are shown three images, each numbered. One is the mark, a series of scratches; two is the brushstroke or the paint; three is a fully rendered rose. *Night Chant Series, Number 3 Dawn* has a beautifully painted, large-scale iris at its center. In this work, color bars, drips, lines or tones of gray become more intrusive on the flower represented. The color bar marches directly across the iris, for example. The artist has united her formal indications of process with the representation of the image itself. Additionally, this work is important as a conceptualization for the artist herself — the missing, but always most important if invisible element in a work of art. Iris is Steir's given first name, Patricia is her middle one, and by choosing to represent this flower, Steir is announcing her presence to us — albeit humorously and ironically.[16]

In the black flower works from 1973, Steir has proceeded, in her exploration of the relationship of representation to abstraction and the relationship of the making of an image to its elements, to construct a symbol, an image which is a symbol of that which it represents, rather than one which is a sign or a signifier. The 1974 paintings acknowledge this transition in her visual language by focusing on the representation of one image — the rose. Steir has said many times that the rose was chosen because its representation is not only a sign of the object it signifies but it can have so many symbolic meanings such as love, blood, a rose by any other name, a rose is a rose is a rose, etc. Much as a lion is a *symbol* of courage, the rose is a *symbol* of various ideas and emotions. The lion however is not a *sign* of courage, nor is the rose a *sign*, in this case, for representation. But in all the 1974 paintings the rose, the symbol, is crossed out by a neat, clear, black X-mark, placed squarely over the rose. This X-mark, unlike those in the pre-1974 works, where it indicates process, here indicates a concept. No, this is not a rose; it is a representation, a symbol, an icon. These paintings contain the most conventional and central issue in painting in the twentieth century: when something is painted so representationally that it becomes a replication of itself, it negates the objecthood of the painting; the painting becomes an icon or symbol for the image.

The 1974 paintings range from the pale and poetic like *Song* and *Moment* to strong, hard works like *Word Unspoken* and *Word*

Unheard. The titles of these paintings are all taken from the poem *Ash Wednesday* by T. S. Eliot. These titles are significant perhaps because of the associations with death, with the beginnings of Lent — a time of spiritual deprivation and preparation for a renaissance, or rebirth. The paintings are very formal, very static. Each contains the crossed out rose, *Word Unspoken* having it as its central and almost sole image; *Word Unheard*, as the center of two horizontal divisions of the canvas. In each case, a few color bars tell us that it is Steir's work, but otherwise the paintings appear anonymous and foreign in the context of her oeuvre. *Moon*, an all black work consisting of a black field divided and punctuated by a silvery grid on which is centered a black rose crossed out with a black X, was the last of these paintings.

In reviewing Steir's work from the early seventies, it is evident that she, like a number of other artists all working in diverse ways, had in common an emphasis on the pursuit of personal and idiosyncratic vision. This emphasis on personal content expressed in a variety of ways, with a variety of means, is why the decade is often called the decade of pluralism, a time when no single style or art movement was identifiable and many different kinds of art-making were in evidence.

However, the flower paintings of 1973 and the rose paintings from 1974 are instances in which Steir's path crossed directly with the interests of a larger community working in a way which was seminal in the development of one identifiable style in art. It has variously been termed "new image, figurative expressionism, primary imagery, emblematic figuration" and the like.[17] Most of these new image or new expressionists themselves would agree that they are the grandchildren of the abstract expressionists and have willingly appropriated either its emphasis on personal content or on the physical process of art-making, and these concerns are central in Steir's work from 1971 to 1974.[18]

In a sense, Steir's conceptions about painting and the visual manifestations of those conceptions paralleled early interest in figuration by other important artists such as Neil Jenney and Robert Moskowitz. However, they proceeded in a more visually obvious direction than did Steir who stopped painting for almost two years. When she did begin to paint and show her work again, the obvious image or recognizable representation was absent. Her ideas and her work had briefly intersected with that of others and then veered away.

Steir did not paint again until 1976. She had reached a dead end in her visual research in painting. The artist has commented, "All the paintings [up to now] were involved with meaning. The meaning of paint, the meaning of language, the meaning of meaning."[19] Steir's exploration of and her research in the way we visually construct ideas from simple marks to complicated representations, had reached a turning point.

Though the artist continued working, she limited herself to drawing and printmaking for the next two years. The dilemma in which Steir found herself in 1974 is best expressed by Eliot's *The Hollow Men:*

> Between the idea
> And the reality
> Between the motion
> And the act
> Falls the shadow.

In her own words, "between the image and the paint, I worked it all out with drawings."[20] Though this important time is discussed thoroughly in *Form Illusion Myth: Prints and Drawings of Pat Steir* published by the Spencer Museum of Art, it is relevant to this discussion to know that in 1975, she began to spend a great deal of time in Europe.[21]

The first trip there was very purposeful. It was, according to the artist, "to start again."

> . . . I went to Amsterdam alone to see the Rembrandts and see the Vermeer. They were really about history and the history of that painting . . . . I seem to see in any great painting, all painting. Especially in Rembrandt again, I see all painting. So those paintings were the death of the icon — of the image — and about painting . . . . I'm interested in the impulse, I'm sure it's not the image . . . . I'm interested in that, so the paintings become about painting, a kind of love; it was also a romance and I suppose the brushstroke is an icon.[22]

Steir ceased drawing and began to work in painting once more after 1976. "Drawing was a long and specific research for me," Steir has remarked, "a form of note-taking."[23] After she stopped drawing, she continued to make lithographs and began to make etchings. The process of making prints now serves for her the same function as drawing used to; it is her most direct form of visual experimentation.

The drawings and prints from the mid-seventies had evolved to a multi-panel format, and this along with other conclusions she arrived at in the graphic work would be the form and the content of the new paintings.

In a one-person show in New York in 1978, she exhibited paintings for the first time since 1975. This exhibition of five paintings completed in 1977 and 1978 included new works which were multi-paneled, consisting of anywhere from two to six equal-size canvases hanging side-by-side and ranging from two to four feet square. Absent were the recurring images of roses, birds, and written instructions to herself, and as one reviewer noted, "The reduced formal vocabulary has made way for more purely painterly . . . expressiveness."[24]

This reduced formal vocabulary was the result of Steir's study of Rembrandt and her conclusions from the research conducted in her drawings. She resolved that in the new works, line would be the only sign of figuration. The same kind of line or mark which was focused on in the center square of the painting would also, used differently, form her characteristic border or frame. The technique employed in these new paintings is informed by that of the old masters; the works of the late seventies are constructed from a painted ground which is drawn into by the artist and the forms are built up by many layers or glazes of paint applied in a planned progression. This way of applying paint is in direct contrast to the *à la prima* or all-at-one-time manner of working which has been most common for artists since the impressionists.

In *Beautiful Painting*, 1977-78, a five-panel work, the first panel is composed of a brown field — obviously produced by the layering of glazes of the primary colors — surrounded by a frame or border. In the center of the painted field, a single brushmark in white is present. Steir's characteristic drips streak downward from this mark. The brushstroke in white, the brushstrokes making up the central field and those forming the border are identical in form and orientation. In the second panel the brown tonality continues and the center is formed by regularly placed rows of white brushstrokes, the border by regularly placed brushstrokes spaced more closely together, forming a field of color, again brown. In the center panel the brushstroke proximity forming the center square and frame are reversed, and in the fourth and fifth all brushstrokes or marks are identical, the center square being differentiated from its border only by the hue of the warm browns and yellow-browns. In the fourth the center is darker in tone than the border, in the fifth this relationship is reversed.

This painting is a lesson in the new vocabulary of the artist and of her reorientation toward a content which is about the artist's mark — the icon of modern art — and about the science of paring painting down to its simplest components, line and color. In a deeper context it is about what Steir calls, "intentionality," a desire of the artist to make a particular mark for a particular reason. The need to make art, to express oneself with the mark, is what art has been about since time of the first man who drew on the wall of a cave to this moment when Steir reduces all art to line and color. In Steir's words,

> They [the 1977-78 works] were kind of love songs to art, in a way, and to artists. They were also about trying to be beautiful and trying to dissect art at the same time. Painting, and at the same time, trying to say, 'This is just a line.' With this impulse, it's art. Given the impulse and the desire, that makes it art.[25]

The painting *Long Chart, Large Chart*, 1977-78, is representative of the same kind of thinking. It is the only work of Steir's which stacks horizontally and which is composed of panels not identical in size. The painting, like *Beautiful Painting*, is about paring things down to the simplest elements of language and picture making — the mark. The only colors used are the simplest — red, yellow, blue, black and white. It is read both horizontally across each panel and then, like a poem, on downward to the next panel. Both these paintings are as Steir has termed it, "either a starting point or an ending point."[26]

As is to be expected in Steir's work, they were yet another starting point. Once the artist had arrived at the mark, or single brushstroke, as a central element in her painting, she executed a series of diptychs in 1979, all, she says, really about Rembrandt. These six large paintings of 1979 continue the square within the square format of the 1977-78 paintings and use various kinds of marks and brushstrokes to evoke a number of contemporary painters' work: Cy Twombly, Willem deKooning, Jackson Pollock, Sol LeWitt and others. This evocation of the work of others is intentional on Steir's part. As before, she is acknowledging her debts to their work and telling us about the act of painting, or as Steir terms it, "intentionality," present in all art. Her 1980 exhibition, *Rembrandt's*

Hairline, in which four of the large diptychs were presented, was characterized in a review which said, "Steir directs us to the twentieth-century realm of the gestural, where abstract markings carry the authority of words and bear the same basic messages about art and life traditionally reserved for representational forms, like those of Rembrandt."[27]

One of these diptychs, *Pencil Painting*, 1979, made with a pencil marking the canvas, is reminiscent of LeWitt's use of systematic wall drawings made with pencil and, in the squareness of the canvas and the center square within a square, his use of the modular unit. In the center of each white square is a single mark. The left-hand panel contains a straight line, the right, a curved one — a series of loops much like a child's writing exercise. Both *Pencil Painting* and *Black and White Painting (After Pollock)*, 1979, are black-and-white works, referring to the restricted color and importance of black and white in both minimal and conceptual art.

Like all Steir's paintings, the 1979 diptychs contain their own irony. The idea of one painter recapitulating another's use of line is satirical and slightly irreverent, as is appropriating another's characteristic gesture and making your own painting from it. Even so these paintings are uniquely Pat Steir's. They are another step in her research about intentionality or desire, and the central marks are a part of Steir's pictorial system dating back to 1972. The characteristic richness of surface present in her work since 1973, and which has been emphasized since 1977, is evident here as well as her continuing interest in process. Much as a child learns to write and draw, she presents us with the beginnings of both language and images, the straight and the curved line. The child's ability to make a shape from straight and curved lines signals readiness for the development of these two communication skills — writing and drawing. They develop concurrently in children, and seem most connected with the ability to abstract and order information. It is not the development of a skill but of a way of thinking which allows the child to employ *signs* which are universally understood as suggesting that for which they are substituted — a thought, and the intention of communicating the thought.[28]

In the paintings from 1977-78, Pat Steir had returned to a child's first attempt at writing or drawing, and broken it down to its most elemental component — the mark. This mark signals an *intent* to make something on a surface. By 1979, she had developed the mark into both the straight and curved line, and, in 1980, like a child's next step, she used these most elemental units of writing and drawing to make a shape. This shape was the diamond and a new interest (or perhaps the reidentification and reconsideration of an old one) enters the work. This was an interest in illusion.

Beautiful American Painting, 1980, is a triptych concerned with illusion. The first panel is composed of a border of yellow brushstrokes surrounding a center field of red. On this field is a dripping brushstroke of blue. The second panel's border is composed of many of Steir's characteristic looping squiggles. In the blue center is a yellow looping line — the line which appeared in the 1979 works. She had used the same stroke in a different size to make the border and the image, or characteristic line in the center field, before. But the third panel, whose border is composed of many diagonal lines crossing each other forming thousands of diamond shapes, has in its center a diamond. With the addition of a few more lines the diamond has been drawn in perspective, given a shadow and has become not only a shape, but a representation of volume. The border colors are again the three primaries and the center is a yellow field drawn on in both red and blue.

With *Beautiful American Painting*, and others from the same period, Steir has returned to representation, but instead of creating a symbol or icon, she has shown us the process by which the artist arrives at the production of an illusion or representation. By this process, she has produced an imitation of reality which is just that — an illusion, not something which is symbolic of reality. If there is an icon it is the mark, and the mark takes its form and meaning from those marks and colors which it exists in relationship to. As in the work from 1972, all parts of the painting take meaning from the other parts of the painting. The third panel of *Beautiful American Painting*, for example, has no meaning, just illusion, if considered by itself. It needs the information in the other panels in order to assume any content.

Beautiful American Painting and other works of 1980 have sometimes been exhibited accompanied by wall installations which consist of drawings related to the painting made by Steir or her assistants directly on the wall. These drawings were first inspired by the ornamentation Steir saw around paintings in the churches and palaces of Europe. The wall installations bespeak a confidence and playfulness on the part of the artist not present in her work since the early seventies. For Steir, the act of drawing on the wall around the works is infinitely satisfying as it gives the paintings an extended context as well as making her feel delightfully mischievous. "It still has for me the element of a forbidden but delightful activity — like a three-year-old who knows you're not supposed to draw on the wall with your crayons, but can't quite resist."[29]

Lima Being (Being/Been), 1980, a nine-panel work which recapitulates the process of making an illusion, is composed of nine relatively small panels. All the parts are set on their corners as diamonds. Steir sees *Lima Being* as one of her works most ideally seen accompanied by a wall installation. The borders of the painting are decorative to an extreme and yet paradoxically are evocative of Mondrian, especially his *Victory Boogie-Woogie*, 1943-44. The panels with their borders or frames, when accompanied by an installation are reminiscent of much art — even, perhaps, the Stations of the Cross, found in the cathedrals of Europe. In each case, the art is installed surrounded by other decorative elements, and both are descriptive, narrative and loaded with symbolic content.

Since the paintings of 1980, Steir has identified and resolved her conflicts about icons, symbols, meaning and the act of painting into an arena rich with possibilities for investigation. In the process she has become a joyful painter whose work reflects her confidence and unrestricted ability, intellectually and technically, to deal with any issue or system of thought. This confidence is reflected in even naming three works from 1981 "icons." *Icon One: The Mother*, *Icon Two: Eros* and *Icon Three: The Boy* are all three-panel works — as will be almost all her paintings since that year.

The artist's resolutions and new fields of investigation are identified and announced in the painting, *Abstraction, Belief, Desire*, 1981, which was preceded by a large etching of the same name. This triptych differs from the *Beautiful American Painting* and other works from 1980, in that the center field has become larger and, while a frame is still present, it no longer is as formally connected to the central image. Additionally, words in a variety of lettering are contained in the borders, both at the top and bottom, and they define and expand the process and intention illustrated in the central field of each panel. In the first panel, a series of Steir's marks, her lexicon, are inscribed along with a circle, square and two diamonds. The words read, *Form* — at the top — *Abstraction* at the bottom. In the second panel, the geometric shapes are rendered in depth; circles become spheres; triangles, pyramids. This panel is accompanied by the words, *Illusion* at the top, and *Belief* at the bottom. The third panel contains a fully rendered image incorporating both lines and geometric shapes in space to produce a picture — an illusion. This picture is accompanied by the words *Myth* and *Desire*.

The painting announces that the myth, which French semiologist Roland Barthes discusses as one result of language, has become unified for Steir with the desire — "intentionality." Walter Benjamin, in an essay called *The Storyteller* discusses myth and the storyteller, who recounts the myth, saying that a myth, unlike simple information, addresses universal concerns and conveys useful information. This usefulness may in one case consist of a moral; in another, some practical advice is given; in a third contains, perhaps, a proverb or maxim. In every case, the storyteller has counsel for others, and Benjamin comments that having counsel for others is less a matter of conveying something specific like an answer to a question, than it is a "proposal concerning the continuation of a story which is just unfolding."[30] The unfolding of the myth, of a visual language of illusion, may be compared to, or used as, a description of the work done in Steir's painting and graphic work since 1981. By putting in front of us the form, the illusion, the myth, the abstraction, the belief, the desire, Steir has set parameters in which she can act to convey a unique and special counsel. In an article from 1973, Marcia Tucker quoted Pat Steir as having stated, "I'm interested in the thing itself, made by me."[31] *Chrysanthemum* and *Joost's Carnation Landscape*, both from 1981, are a strong visual manifestation of this now seemingly prophetic statement.

These paintings, the most purely painterly works produced by the artist, are especially seductive in both the quality of their surface and the beauty of the imagery. Like most all Steir's work they read from left to right and, in the case of *Joost's Carnation Landscape*, in the first panel we are offered Steir's recapitulation in paint of a portion of a flower painting by Edouard Manet. The second panel is a closer view of the two carnations in the background of the first, and in the third, one carnation engulfs the entire panel. In this close-up view, the painting of the petals of the flowers is an energetic cross between the expressionist brushstroke of Van Gogh and the freedom of action found in deKooning's handling of paint. The energy in Steir's painting in these works makes us smile to remember her remark that abstract expressionism seemed "too athletic" to her. These two "flower paintings" are, of course, not about flowers but about order — arbitrary order. One view, the first panel in each case is the form or, in Steir's thinking, the abstraction which produces the most representational image. The second describes the illusion or belief — the need to and process of the ordering of the abstract information into a system which is understood by the self and others. The third panel is the myth and the desire — the myth as a language of art and the desire of the artist as embodied in the primary mark — the brushstroke. Paradoxically and ironically — the close-up view of the image in the first panel is really the most abstract in terms of ordering information. In the most abstract panel, the third, we find the most faithful representation in terms of reality. This panel, however, appears to be the most abstract.

This format and this paradox continue in the most recent paintings in this exhibition, *Cherry Blossoms II (In Winter)*, 1982, and *Morning Trees*, 1983. Both works have an identical image and are based on Van Gogh's painting, *Japonaiserie: The Tree*, 1887. Van Gogh's work was, of course, based on an even earlier visual antecedent, Hiroshige's color woodcut *The Garden of Apricots*, 1856-59. Just after painting *Cherry Blossoms II (In Winter)*, Steir had visited Japan to do a woodcut and became interested in both Japanese screens and Japanese calligraphy. The interest in calligraphy is in keeping with her interest in the mark and its ordering of information into meaning. In *Morning Trees* we see contrasting bands of paint inscribed with calligraphic like marks — a reference to this new interest. Steir discovered as she studied the Japanese screens that a common way of representing, say a bridge, is to draw it three ways, in three aspects or perspectives that indicate the variety of ways in which we see order and understand an illusion. That is, in essence, her concern in these paintings — to indicate order — three kinds of human or arbitrary order — and to marry that concern to perception, intention, myth and beauty. As Barthes has concluded, ". . . this is what we must seek: a reconciliation between reality and men, between description and explanation, between object and knowledge."[32] Pat Steir, in traveling on her own path, has found a special and private place where we are allowed to understand and transcend knowledge about art, ourselves and our world.

Marti Mayo

Notes:

1. This quotation is taken from *Conversation with Pat Steir* by Ted Castle which is included in this publication.
2. Kate Horsfield and Lyn Blumenthal, "Pat Steir," *Profile*, v. 1, no. 6 (Nov. 1981), p. 5.
3. Ibid., p. 2.
4. Ibid., p. 2.
5. Lecture by Pat Steir, Spencer Museum of Art, The University of Kansas, Lawrence, Feb. 5, 1983.
6. *Bird* is not included in this exhibition as it is presumed lost.
7. Marcia Tucker, "The thing itself, made by me." *Art in America*, v. 61, no. 1 (Jan./Feb. 1973), p. 72.
8. Joan Simon, "Pat Steir: Drawings," *Form Illusion Myth: Prints and Drawings of Pat Steir* (Lawrence: Spencer Museum of Art, The University of Kansas, 1983), p. 20.
9. Ibid., p. 21.
10. Tucker, p. 71.
11. Ibid., p. 71.
12. For further discussion on myth and fable as they are used here, please refer to Walter Benjamin, "The Storyteller: Reflections on the Works of Nikolai Leskov," in *Illuminations*, ed. Hannah Arendt (New York: Schocken Books, 1969), pp. 93-109.
13. Steir lecture.
14. John Canaday, "Two Shows South of Houston St.," *The New York Times*, v. 71 (Sept. 30, 1972), p. 27.
15. Steir lecture.
16. Joan Simon makes additional comments on Steir's use of her first name in *Form Illusion Myth: Prints and Drawings of Pat Steir*, cited, note #7.
17. Carolyn Kinder-Carr, *The Image in American Painting and Sculpture 1950-1980* (Akron: Akron Art Museum, 1981), p. 14. The introduction to this catalogue contains a concise and useful description of the ideas which inform both new image and neo-expressionist work.

18. Ibid., p. 14.

19. Steir lecture.

20. Ibid.

21. For further discussion, please see *Form Illusion Myth: Prints and Drawings of Pat Steir*, cited, note #7.

22. Horsfield and Blumenthal, p. 13.

23. Steir lecture.

24. Sarah McFadden, "Pat Steir at Droll/Kolbert," *Art in America*, v. 66, no. 5 (Sept./Oct. 1978), p. 118.

25. Horsfield and Blumenthal, p. 14.

26. Steir lecture.

27. Ronnie H. Cohen, "Pat Steir, Droll/Kolbert Gallery," *Artforum*, v. 18, no. 9 (May 1980), p. 82-83.

28. W. Lambert Brittain, *Creativity, Art and the Young Child* (New York: The Macmillan Co., Inc., 1979), pp. 47-58. In theories about early childhood education, it is generally accepted that scribbling is the first sign of the child's interest in making a mark. The scribbling, composed of both the straight and curved lines, soon becomes organized into attempted, but very abstract, representations of people and things. These first attempts by the child are composed of straight lines and the circle — the first shape to emerge in the child's vocabulary. As the child's ability to think abstractly develops — that is to order information, to codify it into a system which is understood by himself and by others — more shapes enter his vocabulary. The second shape developed for use is usually the square, and by the time a child can make a triangle or diamond, he is ready to *both draw* recognizable images and to *write*.

29. Steir lecture.

30. Benjamin, p. 86.

31. Tucker, p. 71.

32. Roland Barthes, *Mythologies* (New York: Hill and Wang, 1975), p. 159.

Conversation with **Pat Steir**
61 E. 4th Street, February 23, 1982

Over a period of several months in 1981-82, Pat Steir and I had a number of conversations which were meant to prepare me to write the monograph on her complete works to date which appeared in *Artforum* magazine in May 1982. One of these conversations was, we both felt, so remarkable that although only small bits of it found their way into the article, we wanted to publish the whole. As is my normal custom in transcribing the interviews I conduct, I have eliminated the often discursive "questions" which helped to prepare these "answers" and have presented what seems to be a monologue, almost a composition. Pat Steir's words are not her paintings, but she is one of the most intelligent artists in the world, so she deserves to be heard as well as seen.

Ted Castle, April, 1983

Meaning is illusory, which makes meaning marvelous, What I really mean is that meaning is evanescent — that's exactly the word. Philosophy exists only to discover the meaning of meaning, we indulge philosophy, we assume that there's meaning in everything. For the healthy mind it is important to question meaning. Questioning is satisfying, because life ends. Because life ends, meaning can be anything. We have such a short time for discovery and so many different ways for each being to be, philosophy is playing with dread. If I paint a bird with its feathers and the colors of the feathers next to the feathers and break it down five ways the way a bird book does and the way a paint chart does and the way I might too, it's a small perverse playfulness based on dread. The dread of death which is just commonly human — not enough to make you stay in bed every day but looming — we watch death from across the street most times. Especially at our age (forties), and life seems more exhausting because we know we're only halfway through. So finally, I think everything means the same thing. It's all the same thing. Many kinds of believers say it many different ways, but they come to the same conclusion, that it's all part of the same thing, so why not enjoy it? Otherwise life is dreadfully severe, and constantly painful.

The most difficult thing is the perception of one's limitations, of human limitations. Perceiving death comes to us maybe at the age of seven or five, then again at twenty, and certainly again at forty or the mid-thirties. In your forties you begin to perceive life's limitations, which is worse than death, more painful than the perception of death.

Recently I read *The Abyss* by Marguerite Yourcenar, and she says that she writes about men because during the periods of history that she's interested in, women weren't recorded. She says she likes to write about "almost wise men." And what could wisdom be other than accepting what is, whatever you see as being what is. That's why when you meet an older wise person, they always seem jerky, because the perception of what is is always very different for each person. It's really about true value. If you're looking into the subject of meaning, you're looking into the idea of true value. Good and bad, true and false, yes and no, black and white. In youth, particularly a precocious, gifted youth, one sees things very clearly as true and false, yes and no, I can, I can't, I will, I won't, but in time these things become grayer and grayer and more and more alike. I'm not interested at all in the meaning of that, I'm just interested in that it is.

I think the paintings that I love never look finished, whether they're mine or someone else's. They seem always to be very flawed and very vain. I especially love Rembrandt because he was so vain. I love his human vanity. I'm so touched by it, because as he got older he knew about it and his paintings tell you that he knew about it so that instead of becoming dead he became more facile. He became better. His last self-portrait as the apostle Paul is not only a cynical face but it's cynically painted. He could just paint. His painting was as cynical as his face. He was a guy who thought he saw it all and had a tiny bit of hindsight that made the painting great for me. Somewhere in it, he managed to say, "You fool!," to himself. I think that painting is of all the arts the one most related to magic. To attempt to make magic, to make something transcend itself in more than meaning, in spirit. The paintings I love transcend their medium in spirit. The best ones contain something more than what they are. And they're more primitive, I think, than using words. To use paint, to be that limited, is a primitive way to try to transcend anything. The combination of signs and signals makes the magic that can make it transcend what it is. That's really romantic. The whole idea of meaning in art is to transcend particular meaning, to try to deal with meaning is to try to transcend the particular. This is done by addition and subtraction of signs and signals and symbols and skill and lack of skill.

Painting communicates by intention, and the clearer the intention, not the verbal intention, but the desire, the urge, like trying to make gold from mud, is like trying to make meaning from sticky stuff, but I think that no matter what the theory, what the style, even what the meaning is, the urge is always the same. The desire is to leave your mark — not only in painting but in any desire to try to put all those lights out there on the landscape, for instance, into some other moment that will last beyond this moment. It's the desire to say, I was here, I saw, I thought, I felt. The strength of the desire, is about great art; talent is gift — some people can do certain things better than others.

I always like art that fails in some way, that's most human. When I was a child I saw art first in books, in colors that were very off-color, either orange or green depending on the printers, and the way that the photograph was developed. I thought I could never make art because it looked too hard to do. How could I make it all so orange or green? Then my father took me to a museum. He liked Mondrian the best, and that also looked too hard for me to do. I saw a Cézanne painting of a farm boy standing sideways in the doorway and the arm in back was very short and crippled looking and the arm in front seemed too long, it was down to his knee, and when I looked at it it was like eating meat that is too fresh or a turkey egg right from the turkey — it was too shocking, too real. Eighty-day-old eggs from the supermarket are quieter. I was about eleven and the painting was so overwhelmingly moving, so possible, so human. Then I thought that I could do art if all it takes is to be human and not to have to look like Ektachrome. Later when I saw Vermeers in person, I was also amazed at how loose they were — they were nothing at all like the reproductions. They were very composed, and I didn't like them so much, but they were loose, they were a more controlled human, but they were also human. If you got close enough to the surface, you could see that somebody did it, and you could see who he was. Of course doing something very often makes you better at it usually.

I really think that the meaning is the same in the Vermeer and the Rembrandt and the Agnes Martin paintings. The thing that I see in many paintings, and in the urge to make art or write, is a kind of awe. There's religious awe — feeling the universe in terms of God; or there's the awe of the lover — seeing the universe in terms of what someone else seems to make you see; or just the awe of the five-year-old who suddenly notices something that is not himself, he can't eat it, he can't get it. The urge to make anything, to make a poem, to make a sculpture, a painting, no matter how mundane the doer is, it has to do with awe. There's a tree; I think I'll draw a bigger tree right next to it. To add to the general chaos of the universe. To make one more thing that's not part of you. When I was very young I thought that I would like to leave a notebook when I died so somebody could learn from it. Later I realized that that's what novels are! I had stumbled upon the idea of art.

I'm not interested in meaning in a daily way. I'm interested in the way scientists deal with it, in a kind of fake order. I'm interested in many different kinds of arbitrary order. Starting with a mark and bringing it to a figure is one of the kinds of arbitrary order, discovering the fact that figurative and abstract are the same thing. Seeing the mark as the urge and the figure as the collection of marks. A fancier way to express the urge, make it visible. In the flower paintings I did, I first made a painting of a flower and enlarged it until it became a landscape or an abstraction or a universe. Abstraction and figuration are different ways to inspect the same thing — an image and its meaning, or a mark and how it can seem to become an image when it's really just a mark.

When I began making these paintings that show marks, I started with the idea of making a picture of the desire to make a picture. The mark would be the picture, that's all, a kind of primitive picture of desire. I had several fantasies about how children, monkeys, and cave people started to draw and communicate, and how painful the urge must have been before they figured out how to do it. A painful urge about transcending self. It had to do with transcending isolation. It's only my fantasy, but I have a feeling that it's close to the truth. A symbol calls up a recollection that almost has to do with communication. Almost because communication has to do with meaning and meaning slips away. So I guess we love the people that we can almost communicate with. We can almost understand.

I think that scientists do these things the same way that artists do it — by imposing an arbitrary order or the appearance of meaning on things — but when laypeople think of science they suppose an absolute order, an absolute system. Finally it's all expressionism, basically everything is expressionism. We flounder around looking for something or trying to communicate something, it's either a search or a telling. If you look at art in the past several years, in a way it all slips into expressionism so quickly but science is expressionism too because the idea of what he's going to try to find has to occur to the scientist. And they say that occurs in their presleep state. That is it comes from the unconscious. Having decided what they're looking for, then they make their search, often finding things they never knew existed and that they certainly weren't searching for. I have a good friend who is a DNA researcher, and he has many artist friends. He's gifted as a scientist because he's very relaxed, he doesn't set out to find much — he sets up a problem and then finds whatever he can, whatever turns up in the analysis of the problem. So he may be looking for why there is a kind of epilepsy and then discover a whole new virus which he wasn't looking for at all. The only reason he's doing anything of this sort is to see if they can find a biological medicine, but he's not thinking about why he's doing it. So he's like an artist, in a way, in a big way. After finishing something, artists often say, well, I was looking for such and such. Scientists also know that one and one are always one and one. They are never two because the two is a third thing. An artist will perhaps make a line and then look at it and say, well, I really like that line. I don't regard this as accidental at all. It has to do with that unconscious, and the unconscious isn't accidental. If you think clearly about a problem you limit the solution by what you thought in the first place. But if you can possibly relax, there's always a surprise solution that occurs to you. It's not accidental or intuitive — a guess — but it's from the place that real knowledge is. Intuitive implies, "from the Gods," from outside yourself. But if you can relax, things just rise up from the unconscious. It's much easier in art than in life to have that happen. That's what people go through analysis for — to see what they're thinking. If you set up a problem to solve in a painting, the only way to solve it is to solve it through several approaches at one time. My idea is that a given work is only part of a body of work rather than a unique, independent, finished work.

For at least ten years I've had the same subject matter and then before that, as a child, I had the same subject matter, the same marks and images. My mother has a drawing I did when I was eight years old, ink blots on a piece of paper. It's the piece of paper next to the piece of paper I was drawing on where the ink was so I wouldn't stain my desk and my room, and that piece of paper got marks and stains on it and I turned all those marks and stains into figures and threw away the drawings. My mother has that in a frame, it is one of the few things she kept from the past. I don't know if she will loan it to me to show, but I'd like to show it in my print and drawing show. I was a little girl when I did it but it looks like I could have done it yesterday. My subject matter is always the same and it's always really about illusion, and the illusion of meaning. The images that come up have to do with the images changing in time — at different times in your life there are different things that you are preoccupied with. When I painted the rose paintings in 1974, I chose the rose because it could mean so many things. It had so many solid daily associations. Like the rose is a rose is a rose, and there are lots of songs, so I chose the rose because it could mean so much. Then I crossed it out in all the paintings because it was always a central image or a double image on a divided canvas. I was making jokes about making white paintings, and those paintings were always black or white and the rose was always red or white. So I thought, if I make an image and cross it out then there's no image in the painting, it's a white painting, but it looks like a crossed-out rose. Also the rose is an icon, and at that time I was interested in getting rid of the icon. In some paintings I paint it out in such a way that it would peek through.

It's like the idea of arriving at white, to arrive at nirvana, say. To do that you have to cross out or wear out a lot of things. Those paintings have other meanings as well. All of them are named from the poem *Ash Wednesday* by T.S. Eliot. The poem is very laden with Christian symbolism, and it can be taken many ways, so putting a very romantic image like the rose in it and crossing it out and calling it "Speak to the Wind, to the wind only, for only the wind will listen," brings up the complicated meanings of silence and the complicated not silence of something withheld. To put it there and take it away shows that it's being withheld. That was very particular to those paintings. You can never remove an incident from life. So I thought that I would at least make them lifelike. If I didn't want to retract any statements I didn't cross anything else out.

Recently I crossed something out again, but in earlier paintings I worked on them like a diary. I was very involved with John Cage's music and the idea that he presented you with a limited amount of chaos for a certain time. In some ways I was very naive artistically, very naive about the time that I was in, in those first paintings that I did a lifetime ago now. I thought that I would make a visual chaos or try to make a visual chaos, so when something happened in a painting that I didn't like I just crossed it out and went on. I thought it would be very lifelike, crossing out and continuing. Rather than removing things, obliterating them. Later on I found that I couldn't make chaos, I found that I could only make symmetry.

This last year, I crossed out the boy in the series of three triptychs to make the painting more violent. It was a painting of an assistant I had who was movie-star beautiful and I hadn't painted a portrait in years but he was so handsome that I wanted to paint him, and also I wanted to make a painting he could understand. His generation is so warlike, I think, not only warlike but terrified of war, and this I know because of young artist friends and many of them are preoccupied with the end of the world. I think that's why there is so much figurative painting because there is always figurative painting when people are worried about the end of the world. There was expressionist figurative painting before both world wars. In this century it is a prewar tendency, if not before. We need something to recognize readily, there is no time to investigate things "abstractly." We are a generation between wars. We had a very leisurely and optimistic education because the war had just ended. Whereas now I think that people force themselves to become adults, they don't linger. I lingered all through my twenties in a kind of adolescent way. I worked and had troubles but never thought of myself as having to hurry, only to work to pay the rent, but not having to hurry to develop especially quickly as a painter. I dallied in other fields, and I think many people in our generation did that. I feel the same sense of panic that young people feel now, but I don't think as they do, because the way I think is set in terms of my leisurely education. Anyway I tried to paint the boy in a way he could understand and he did. He said, "Oh look. I'm on an antiwar poster!" And I asked him, "What period of art do you think this is like?" And he said, "I don't know." It was like a Fauve painting because of the color and violence.

At times I have played with the ideas or the style of certain artists who I know — I feel that if I love it, it is mine. It's not grabbing it, it's playing with it. Because I think that all art is the same thing, I think that I can use it playfully. In the earliest work I showed, that was just what I did. I would make one area as close as I could get to remind one of a Brice Marden waxy surface. I did an etching called *Between the Lines*. It was a grid with notations on the bottom such as birds and acorns and other things, and this was for Agnes Martin — it was between her lines, like a playful, friendly letter to her. Saying I read between your lines. I know what you said. You said sky and rocks and so on. For me many of her canvases were very much like landscapes and incredibly touching as landscape meditations, and I found them to be expressionist paintings done by a very quiet person. I saw her as I saw Rembrandt or anyone else in history; I put her in history, although she was contemporary. I know a lot of people think that the drips in my work are about Jasper Johns, but I went to art school with Brice Marden and he used to leave a line where he taped it and the underpainting showed through and I loved that very much. I used to sit and watch him work rather than doing my own work. I always felt and later noticed that Robert Ryman's white paintings, his early ones, were always painting over something else. Whenever I paint white over something I think of him. I think of arriving at white rather than beginning with white. It's different with Sol LeWitt. At the time when he was making lines for a very specific place and defining them very exactly, I, on the contrary, would make a line that was nowhere. He and I have precisely a different idea. His lines were very specific and logical, and my lines were mad marks. I think that when I made a line in the middle of a page framed by many lines like itself I meant it as an impulsive mark, as subjective. His view was that his line was not an illusion. I meant that my lines were an illusion — a symbol.

I think that a straight line is what the monkey made, an impulse, and the curved line is man-made, desire. People who study children's drawings think that children start just scribbling around then they start to make a round moon, then they draw a triangle, and that means they can deal with abstractions. I use that in a lot of my work. Signs on top of whatever else, signs hanging above what I did below it. My idea is that the figurative image is more abstract than the straight line or the curved line because it requires more abstract thinking. We keep feeling always that we're arriving someplace, so then we think an abstraction is more abstract than an image because we only recently dared to think of it as anything at all other than a patch of paint. I think if you make a piece of blue and a piece of red it's just a piece of blue and a piece of red. But if you make it a blue sky and a red sea, it is a very complicated gestural thought pattern. Children's drawings are all non-figurative at first but when they become more competent verbally they start to make little triangles out of the scribbles and so on. I'm not trying to prove a point, though, I just think that since I have so much trouble understanding what I'm seeing happening before me, I might as well amuse myself by thinking about it, playing with it. Playing with the idea of reality. Not playing with reality and truth, but with the idea of reality, with what seems like truth. Figurative seems like truth for the figurative painter and abstract seems like truth for the abstract painter but if they seem the same then neither seems like truth.

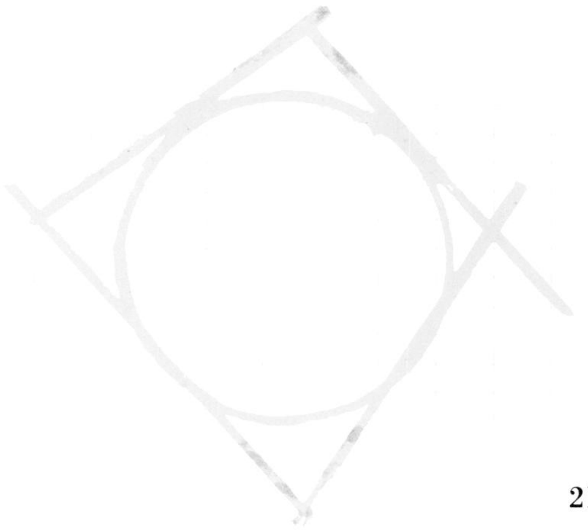

Some years ago, I was moving from one place to another, and I carelessly destroyed some of my paintings from years ago, I didn't feel like carrying them with me anymore. I didn't think they were good; I didn't care what happened to them. I do that with many things I have. I keep very few things. I'm careless with them. They're in my way. I didn't throw them out because of trying to control other people's view of me historically. When I look at the pictures of them, I think they're very good, but at the time I thought — I can make better ones. After that, after I started showing regularly in 1971 or so, I sold all of the paintings I made so they're safe in other peoples' hands. They take care of them because they invested money in them. I do love seeing old paintings of mine in somebody's house or in a gallery or a museum; it's like stumbling on the work of a person I used to know. But to live with them is like hanging your own past on the wall. It's living in the past. I also don't like to force people to comment on my work.

The thing I like about semiologists is the way they feel free to discuss anything. They feel they can study the form, structure and signs of anything at all. I do the same thing in my painting. I feel free to study, that is to paint anything. When you read the work of semiologists, often they write about things they know nothing about. They study it. They're sort of tourists in the world of phenomena, in the world of meaning. The trouble with it is that it has become academic, and boring. I know a woman who is eighty-eight years old, a psychiatrist, and she said, "Oh, yes, Lacan was very interesting but he went a little off, don't you think? He was a nice boy but he really got carried away." When there's a second or third generation of something, it becomes like a religion and very boring. At first it's entertaining then it's boringly religious. When unskilled labor studies something serious, it's dangerous! It's the end of philosophy when it becomes academic.

I like the idea of conceptual art a lot. I disagree that it is conceptual — I think it is subjective. So I play with its subjectively. More obviously full of hot air. I want it to be funny if I can. I love it when people laugh at my pictures. I don't think that the flower paintings I did last year were funny, they were just high romance.

I feel that certain kinds of images are mine. In the first set of paintings, I did the bird. If I see a bird in any image at all, even in the Audubon bird book, I think that it is mine. The rose and the iris. When I do an iris I think of it as a self-portrait because Iris is my secret first name. The rose because I've painted it so often. And the color cards that they put up next to painting when they photograph paintings, I think they're mine too. And the silhouette of a certain kind of rolling mountain which I probably only used in a few paintings. And then the drippy mark. I don't feel intensely identified with any one image. In the past I was interested in the images because I was interested in meaning. Now I'm more interested in illusion, and the flower paintings are about that. Recently when I was looking at seascapes at the Louvre, I noticed that when you stand across the room they look like seascapes and when you stand very close to them they look like paint. Now I'm interested in illusion, in the last sequence of paintings, and in the second half of life. It's elusive.

Ted Castle

Catalogue of the **Exhibition**

All dimensions are in inches, height preceding width.

Looking for the Mountain 1971
Oil, crayon, pencil and ink on canvas
108 × 72
Collection Richard M. Hollander, Kansas City, Missouri

The Answer for Anita and Leibnitz 1972
Oil, crayon, pencil and ink on canvas
94½ × 72
The Art Museum, Princeton University; (gift of Leonard H. Bernheim, Jr.)

Border Lord 1972
Oil and pencil on canvas
72 × 108
Collection Ponderosa Inc., Dayton, Ohio

Cellar Door 1972
Oil, crayon, pencil and ink on canvas
72 × 108
Collection Mr. and Mrs. Victor W. Ganz;
courtesy Max Protetch Gallery, New York, New York

The Four Directions of Time — No. 2 Entropy 1972
Oil on canvas
84 × 72
Dallas Museum of Fine Arts; gift of Shaindy Fenton

Three Green Days 1972
Oil, crayon, pencil and ink on canvas
72 × 108
Collection Mr. and Mrs. Anthony J. A. Bryan

Black 1973
Oil and pencil on canvas
72 × 132
Collection Steven D. Robinson

Breadfruit 1973
Oil, crayon and pencil on canvas
84 × 84
Collection Martin Melzer

Line Lima 1973
Oil, crayon and pencil on canvas
84 × 84
Lent by the Whitney Museum of American Art, New York;
Anonymous gift, 1974

Night Chant Series, Number 3 Dawn 1973
Oil, crayon and pencil on canvas
84 × 84
Collection Mr. and Mrs. S. I. Newhouse, Jr.

Moon 1974
Oil on canvas
84 × 84
Collection the Eason Gallery, Santa Fe, New Mexico

Word Unheard 1974
Oil on canvas
84 × 84
Albright-Knox Art Gallery; promised gift of Mr. and Mrs. Armand J. Castellani

Word Unspoken 1974
Oil and pencil on canvas
72 × 72
Anonymous loan

Beautiful Painting 1977-78
Oil on canvas
5 panels, each 24 × 24
Collection Vera Q. List

Long Chart, Large Chart 1977-78
Oil on canvas
4 panels; top to bottom, $13\frac{1}{2} \times 93\frac{1}{4}$, $13\frac{1}{2} \times 95$, 17×103, 17×114
Collection Mr. and Mrs. Laughlin Phillips

Black and White Painting (After Pollock) 1979
Oil on canvas
2 panels, each 72×72
Private collection

Pencil Painting 1979
Pencil on canvas
2 panels, each 72×72
Courtesy Wadsworth Atheneum; Sol LeWitt collection

Beautiful American Painting 1980
Oil on canvas
3 panels, each 60×60
Private collection

Lima Being (Being/Been) 1980
Oil on canvas
9 panels, each $23\frac{3}{4} \times 23\frac{3}{4}$
Collection The Chase Manhattan Bank

Abstraction, Belief, Desire 1981
Oil on canvas
3 panels, each 60×60
Collection The Prudential Insurance Company of America

Chrysanthemum 1981
Oil on canvas
3 panels, each 60×60
Collection Gloria and Leonard Luria

Icon One: The Mother 1981
Oil on canvas
3 panels, each 48×48
Courtesy the artist and Max Protetch Gallery, New York, New York

Icon Two: Eros 1981
Oil on canvas
3 panels, each 48×48
Courtesy the artist and Max Protetch Gallery, New York, New York

Icon Three: The Boy 1981
Oil on canvas
3 panels, each 48×48
Courtesy the artist and Max Protetch Gallery, New York, New York

Joost's Carnation Landscape 1981
Oil on canvas
3 panels, each 60×60
Sydney and Frances Lewis Collection

Painting for 1984 1981
Oil on canvas
3 panels, each 42×42
Private collection

Cherry Blossoms II (In Winter) 1982
Oil on canvas
3 panels, each 60×60
McIntosh/Drysdale Gallery, Houston, Texas

Morning Trees 1983
Oil on canvas
3 panels, each 60×60
Courtesy the artist and Max Protetch Gallery, New York, New York

Color Plates

All dimensions are in inches, height preceding width.

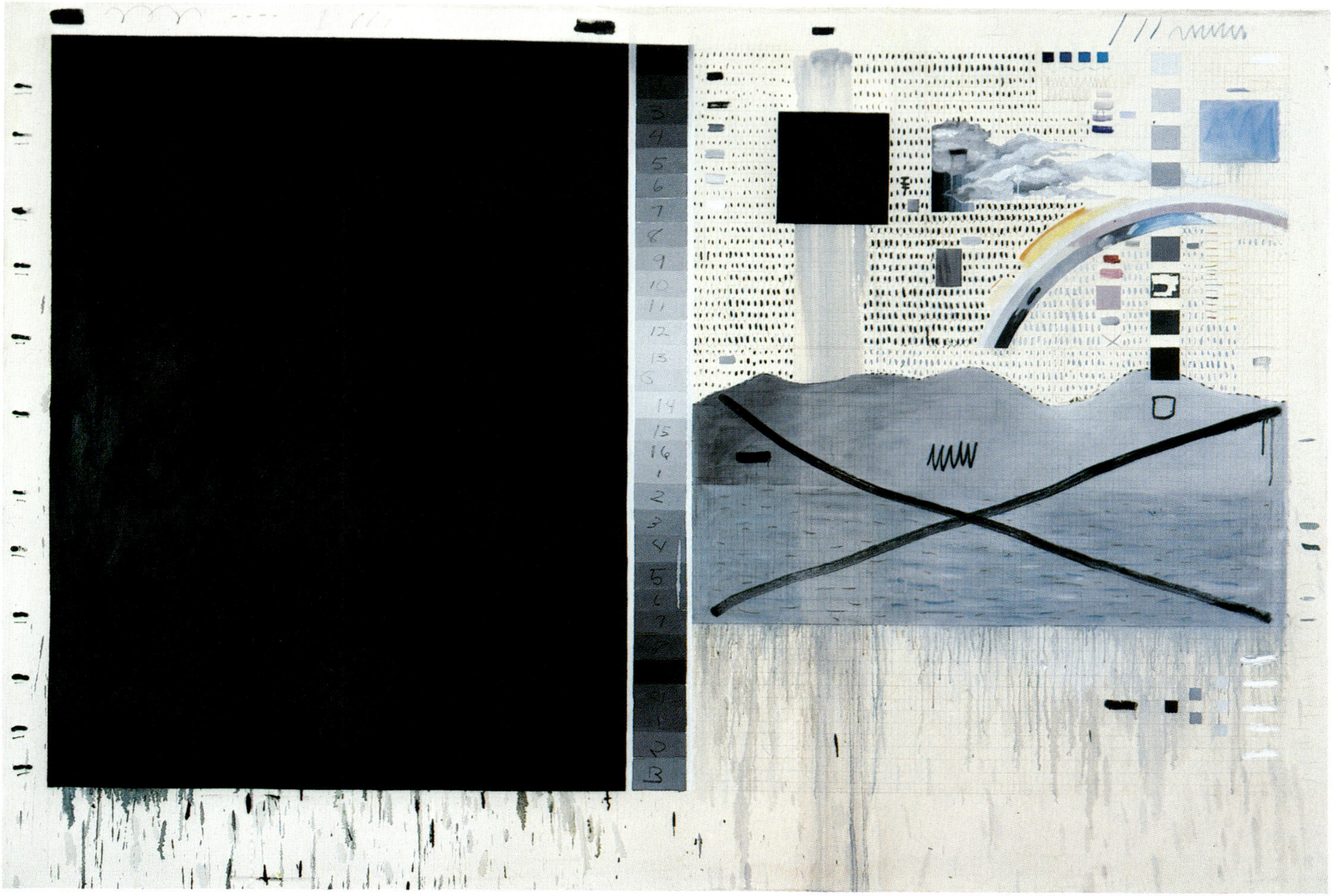

Cellar Door 1972
Oil, crayon, pencil and ink on canvas
72 × 108
Collection Mr. and Mrs. Victor W. Ganz;
courtesy Max Protetch Gallery, New York, New York

Line Lima 1973
Oil, crayon and pencil on canvas
84 × 84
Lent by the Whitney Museum of American Art, New York; Anonymous gift, 1974

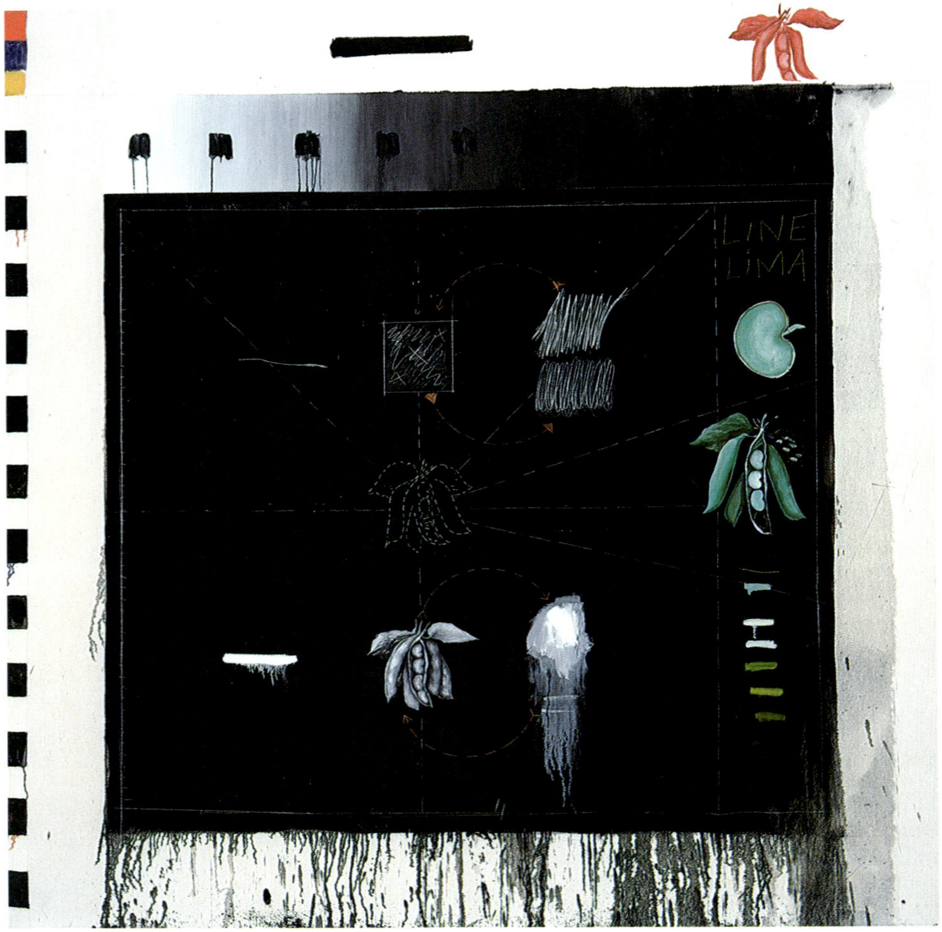

Breadfruit 1973
Oil, crayon and pencil on canvas
84 × 84
Collection Martin Melzer

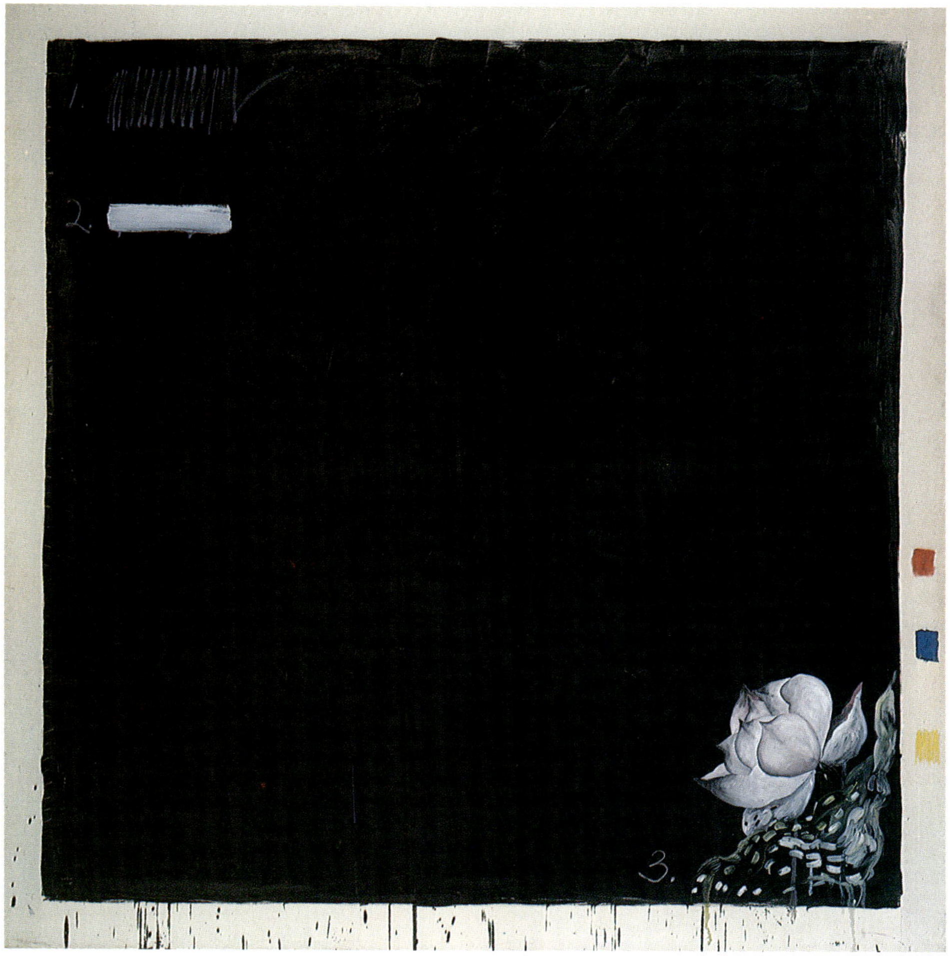

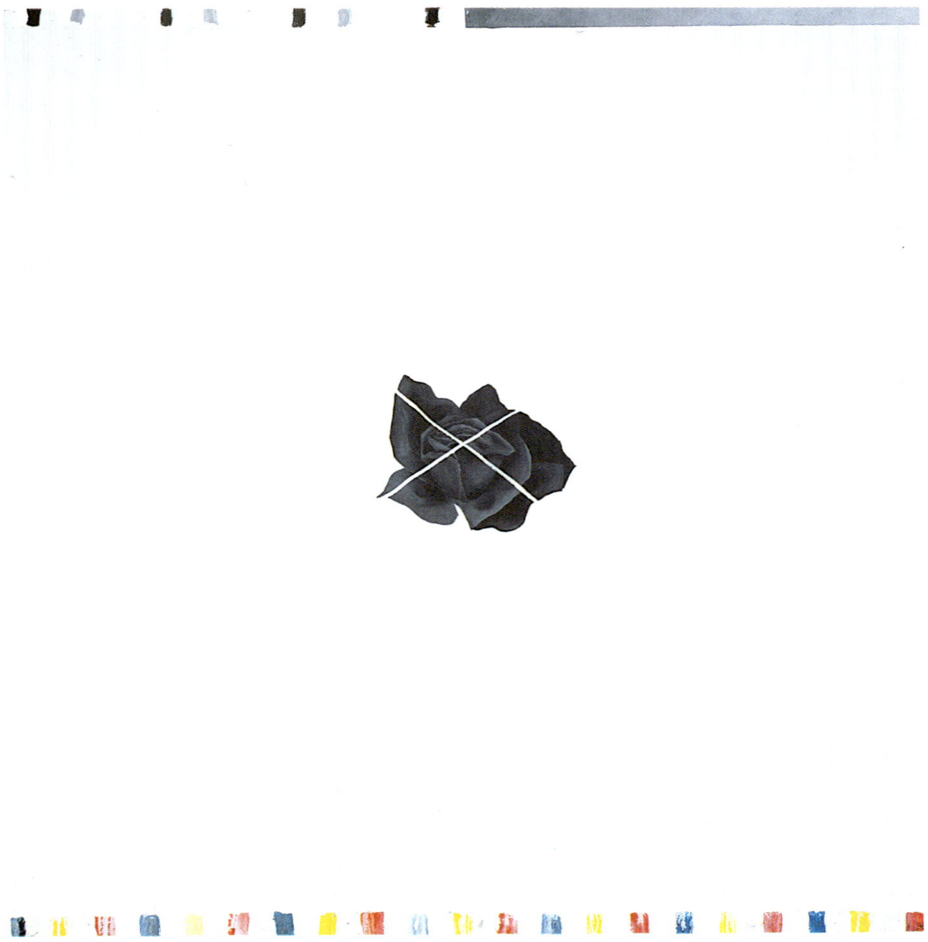

Word Unspoken 1974
Oil and pencil on canvas
72 × 72
Anonymous loan

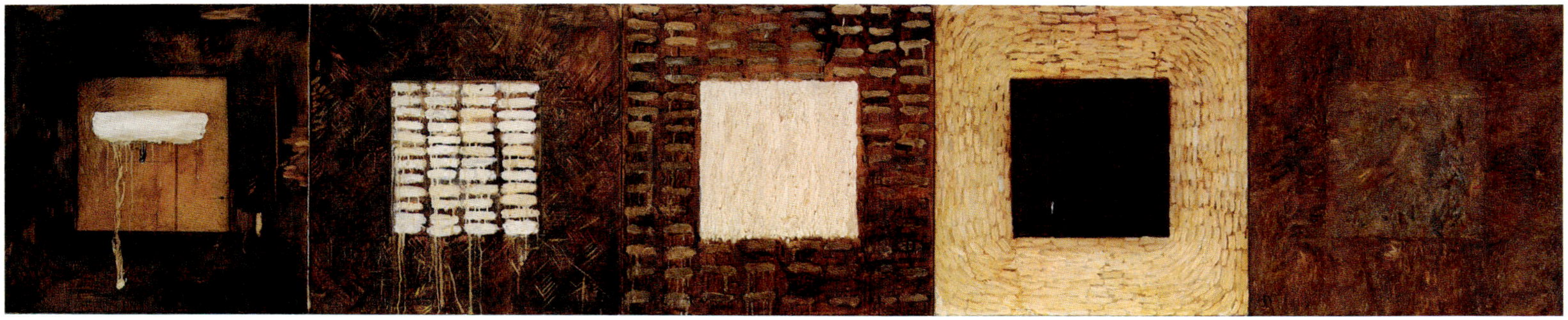

Beautiful Painting 1977-78
Oil on canvas
5 panels, each 24 × 24
Collection Vera Q. List

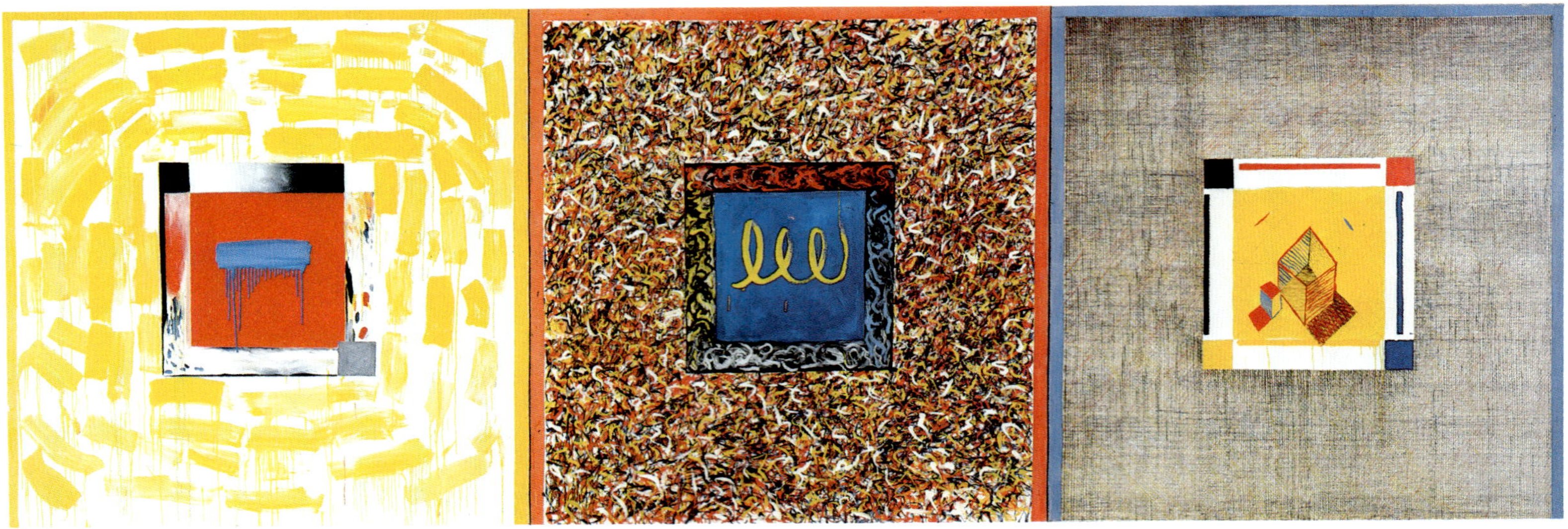

Beautiful American Painting 1980
Oil on canvas
3 panels, each 60 × 60
Private collection

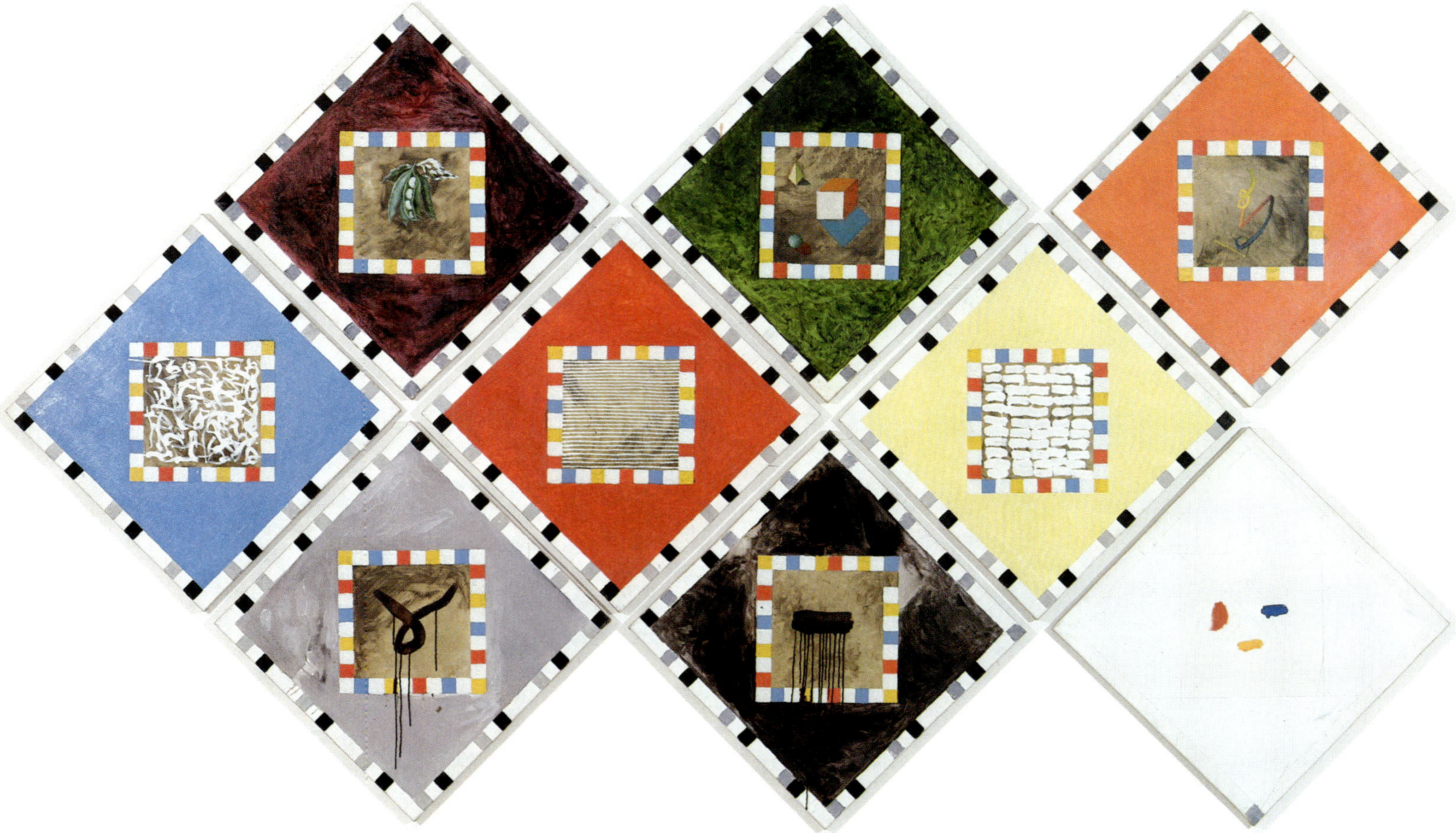

Lima Being (Being/Been) 1980
Oil on canvas
9 panels, each $23^{3}/_{4} \times 23^{3}/_{4}$
Collection The Chase Manhattan Bank

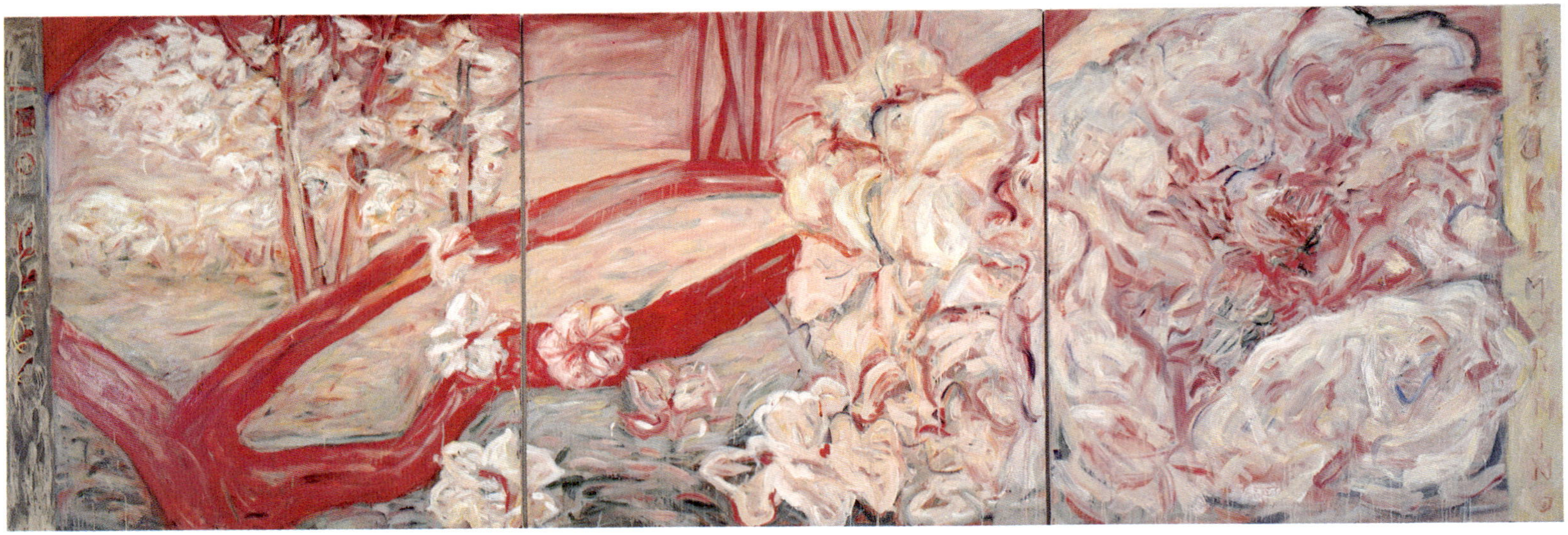

Morning Trees 1983
Oil on canvas
3 panels, each 60 × 60
Courtesy the artist and Max Protetch Gallery, New York, New York

Black and **White Plates**

All dimensions are in inches, height preceding width.

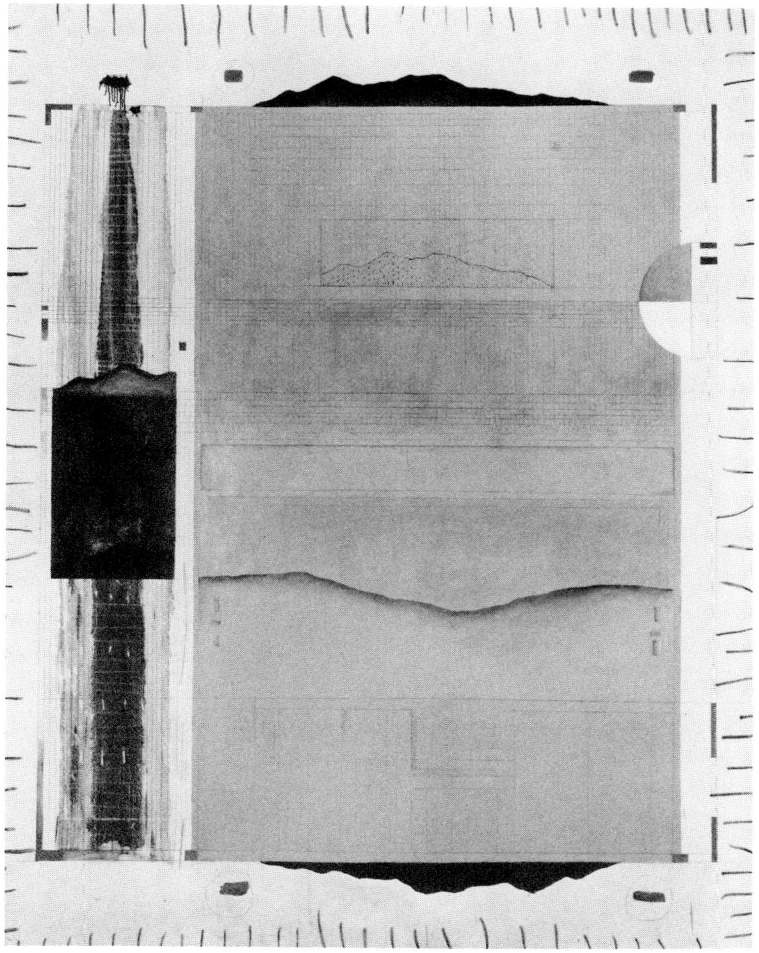

Looking for the Mountain 1971
Oil, crayon, pencil and ink on canvas
108 × 72
Collection Richard M. Hollander, Kansas City, Missouri

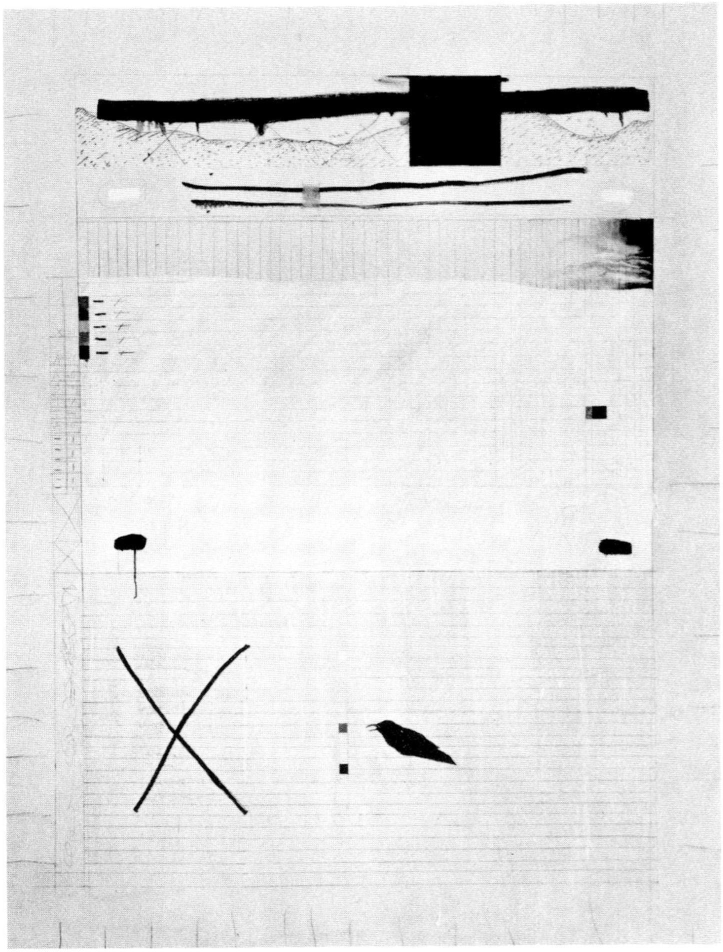

The Answer for Anita and Leibnitz 1972
Oil, crayon, pencil and ink on canvas
$94\frac{1}{2} \times 72$
The Art Museum, Princeton University; (gift of Leonard H. Bernheim, Jr.)

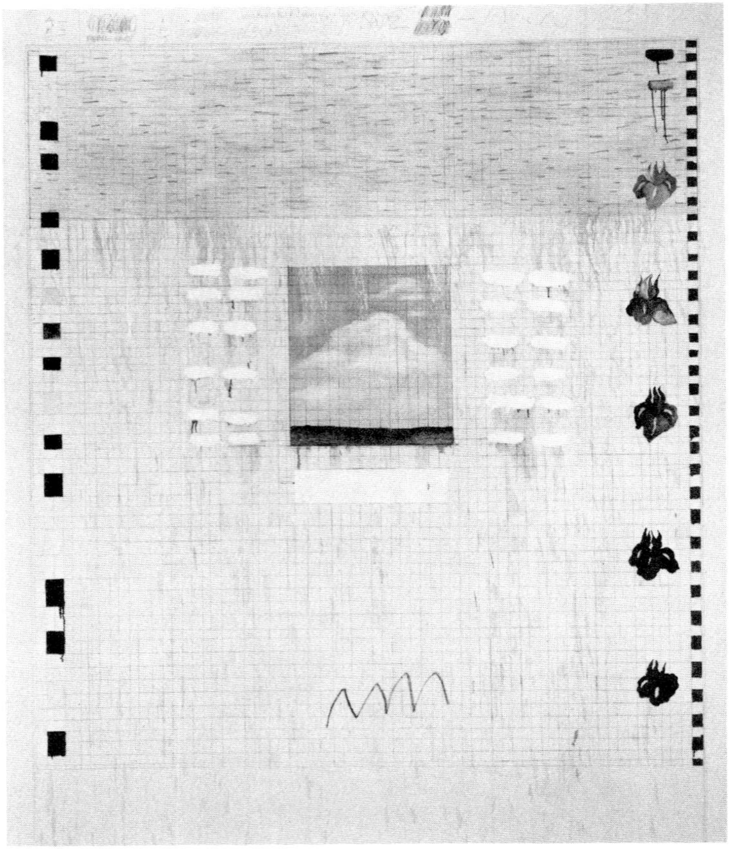

The Four Directions of Time — No. 2 Entropy 1972
Oil on canvas
84×72
Dallas Museum of Fine Arts; gift of Shaindy Fenton

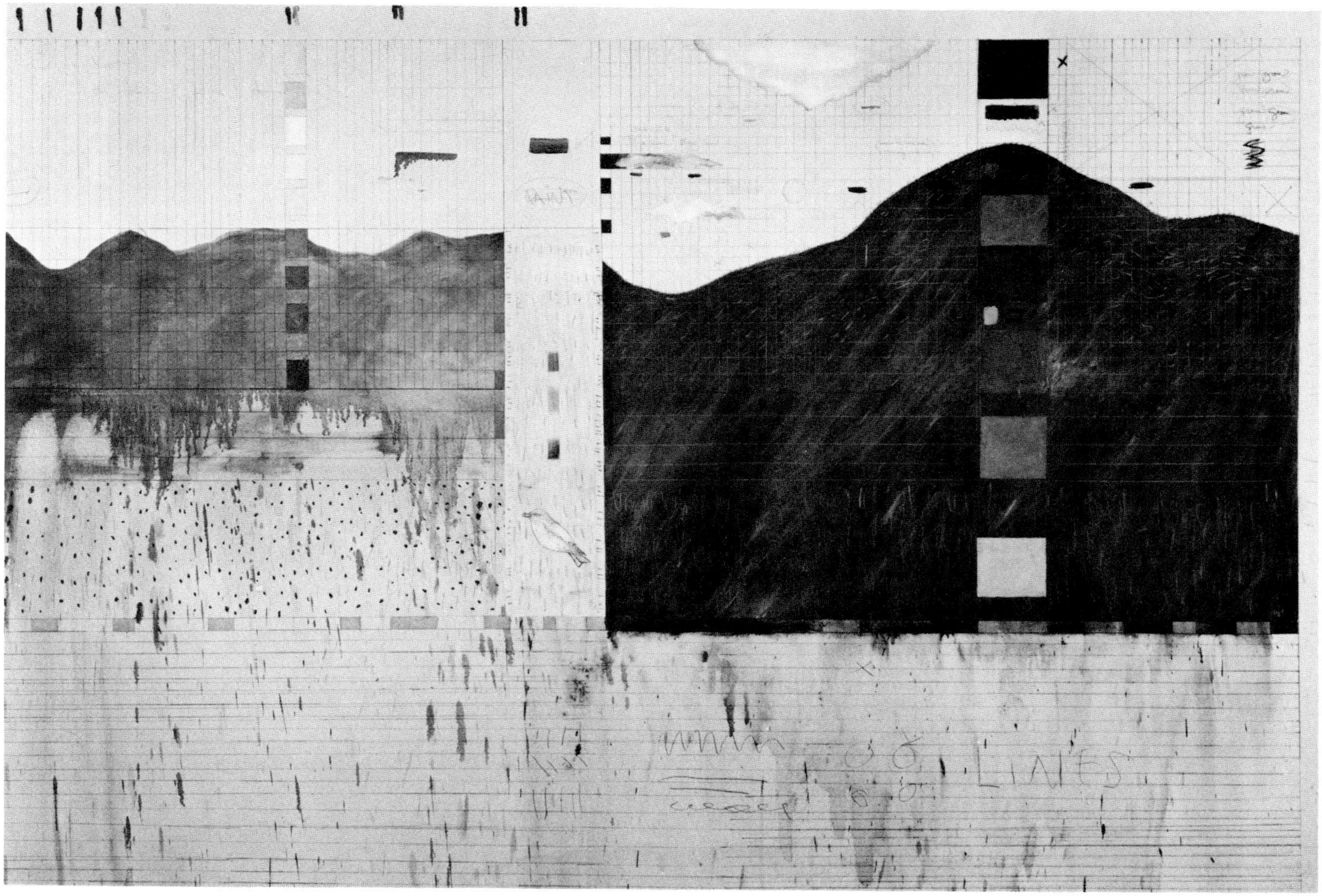

Three Green Days 1972
Oil, crayon, pencil and ink on canvas
72 × 108
Collection Mr. and Mrs. Anthony J. A. Bryan

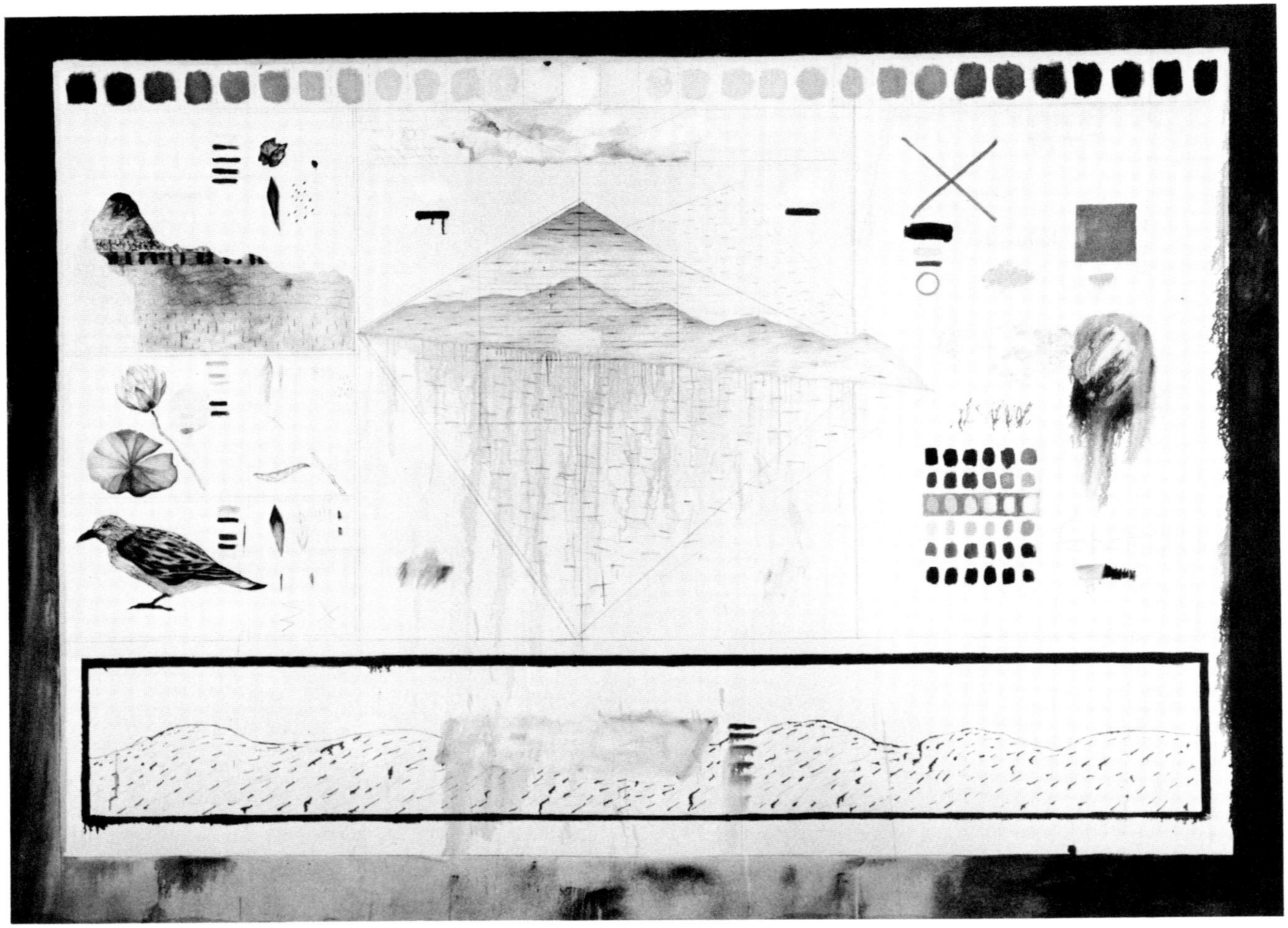

Border Lord 1972
Oil and pencil on canvas
72 × 108
Collection Ponderosa Inc., Dayton, Ohio

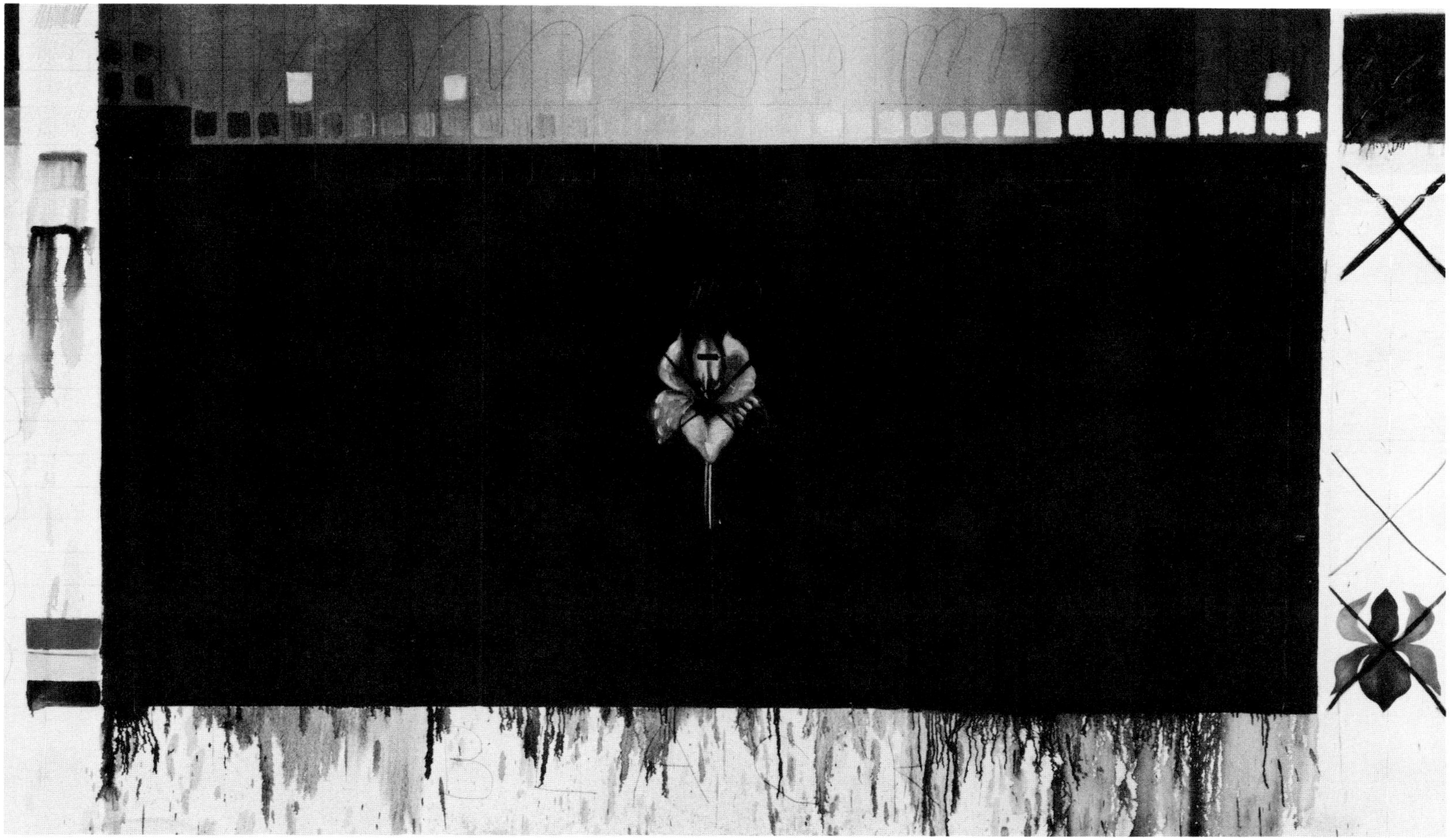

Black 1973
Oil and pencil on canvas
72 × 132
Collection Steven D. Robinson

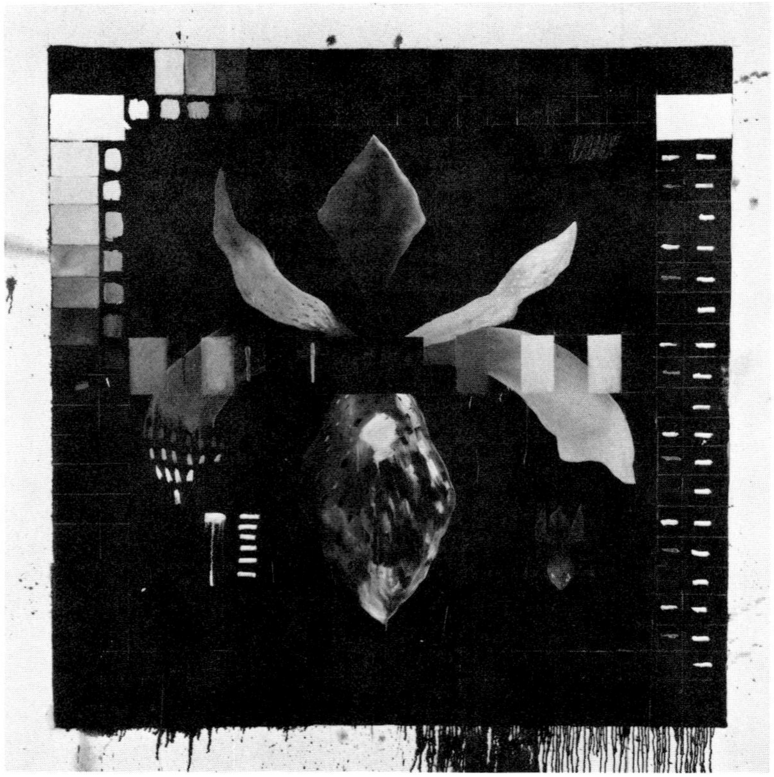

Night Chant Series, Number 3 Dawn 1973
Oil, crayon and pencil on canvas
84 × 84
Collection Mr. and Mrs. S. I. Newhouse, Jr.

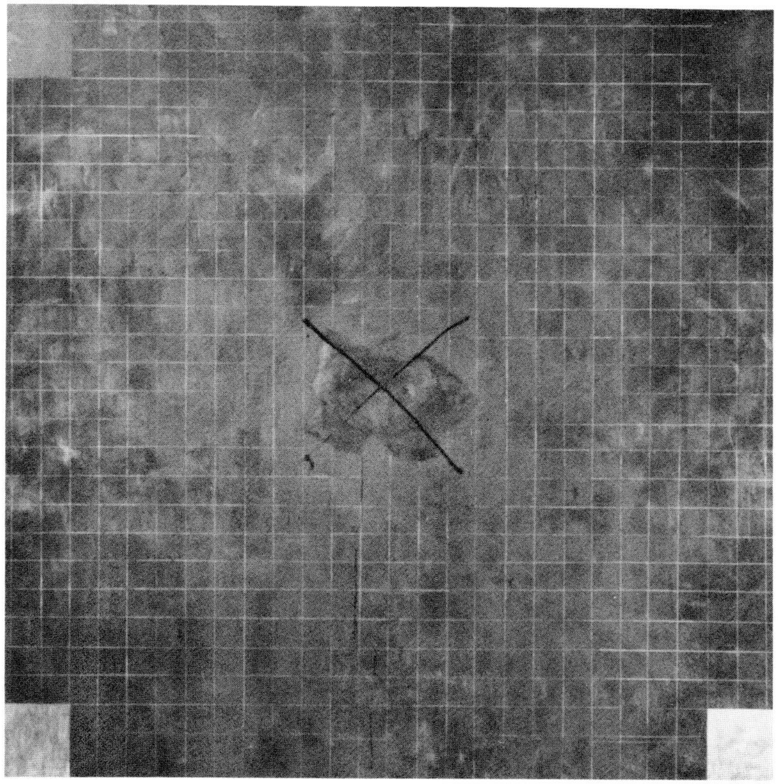

Moon 1974
Oil on canvas
84 × 84
Collection the Eason Gallery, Santa Fe, New Mexico

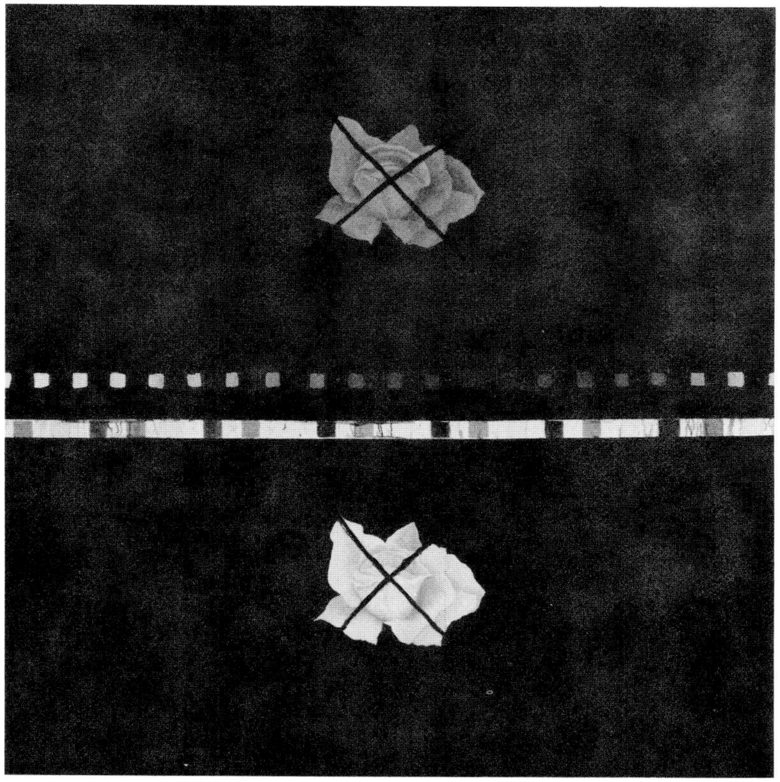

Word Unheard 1974
Oil on canvas
84 × 84
Albright-Knox Art Gallery; promised gift of Mr. and Mrs. Armand J. Castellani

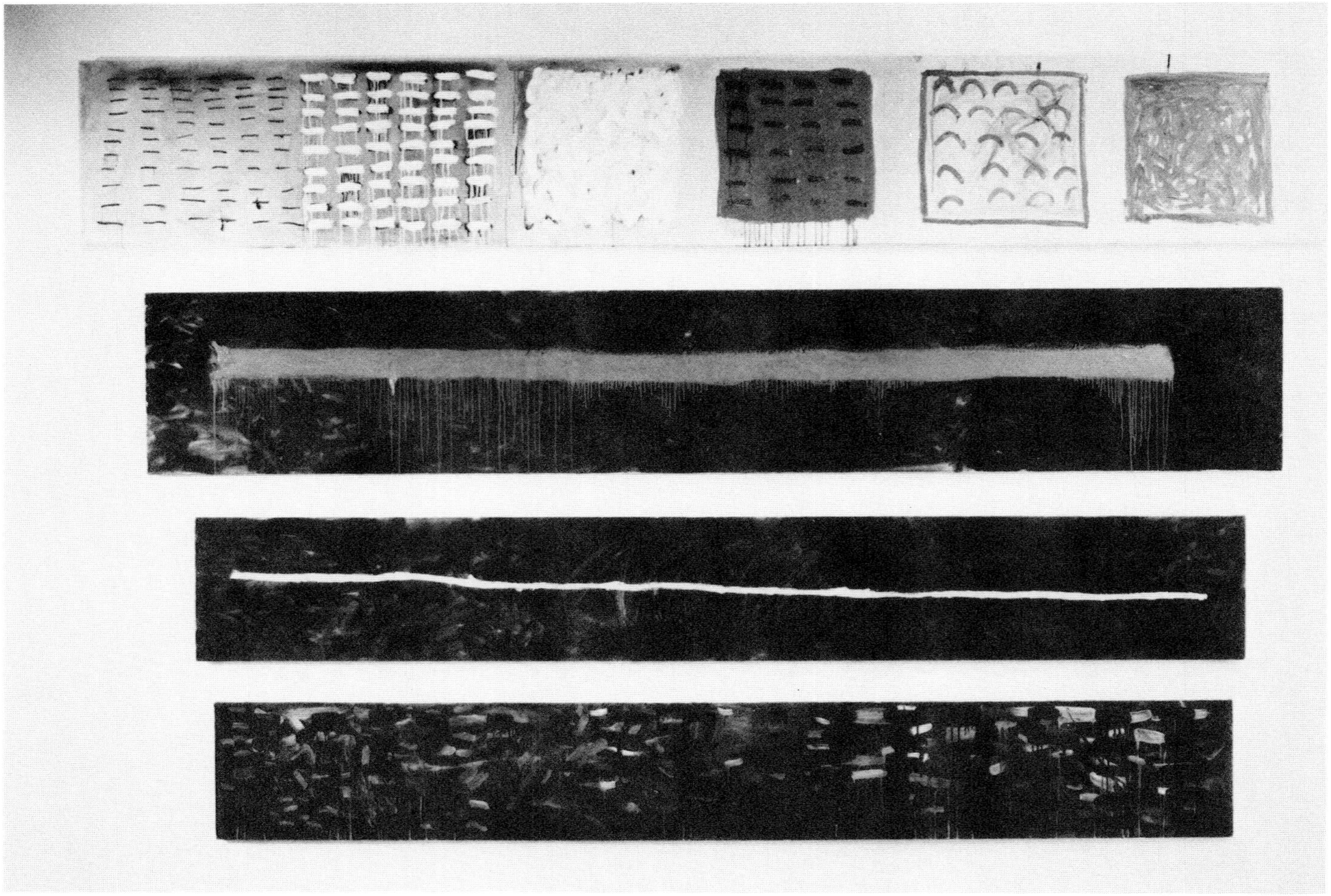

Long Chart, Large Chart 1977-78
Oil on canvas
4 panels; top to bottom, $13\frac{1}{2} \times 93\frac{1}{4}$, $13\frac{1}{2} \times 95$, 17×103, 17×114
Collection Mr. and Mrs. Laughlin Phillips

Pencil Painting 1979
Pencil on canvas
2 panels, each 72 × 72
Courtesy Wadsworth Atheneum; Sol LeWitt collection

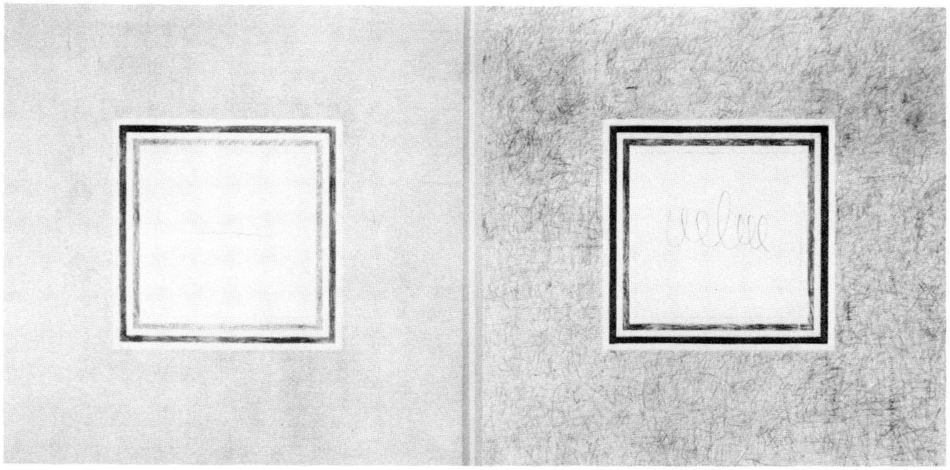

Black and White Painting (After Pollock) 1979
Oil on canvas
2 panels, each 72 × 72
Private collection

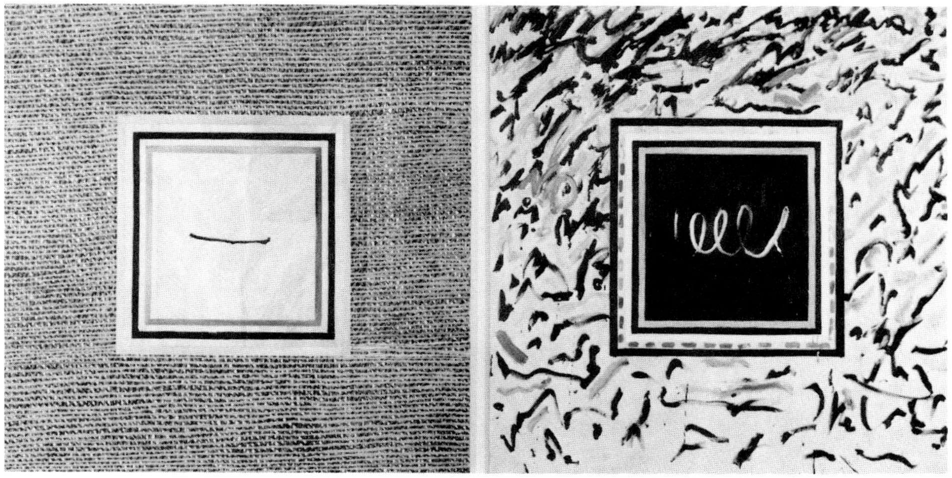

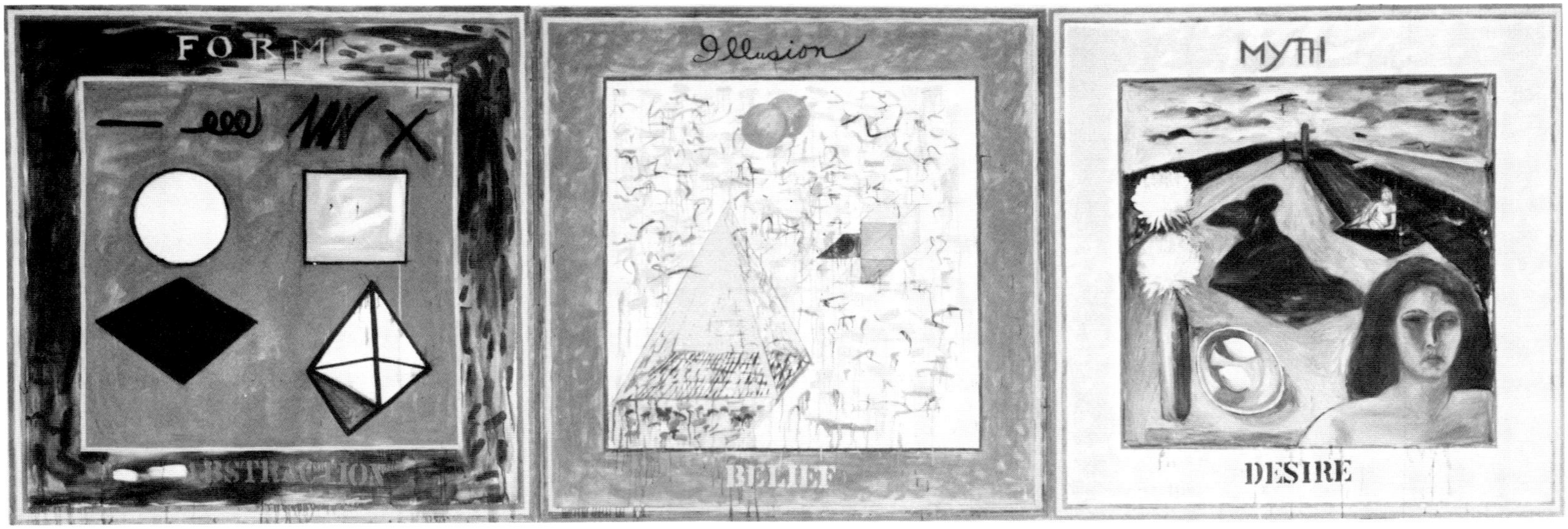

Abstraction, Belief, Desire 1981
Oil on canvas
3 panels, each 60 × 60
Collection The Prudential Insurance Company of America

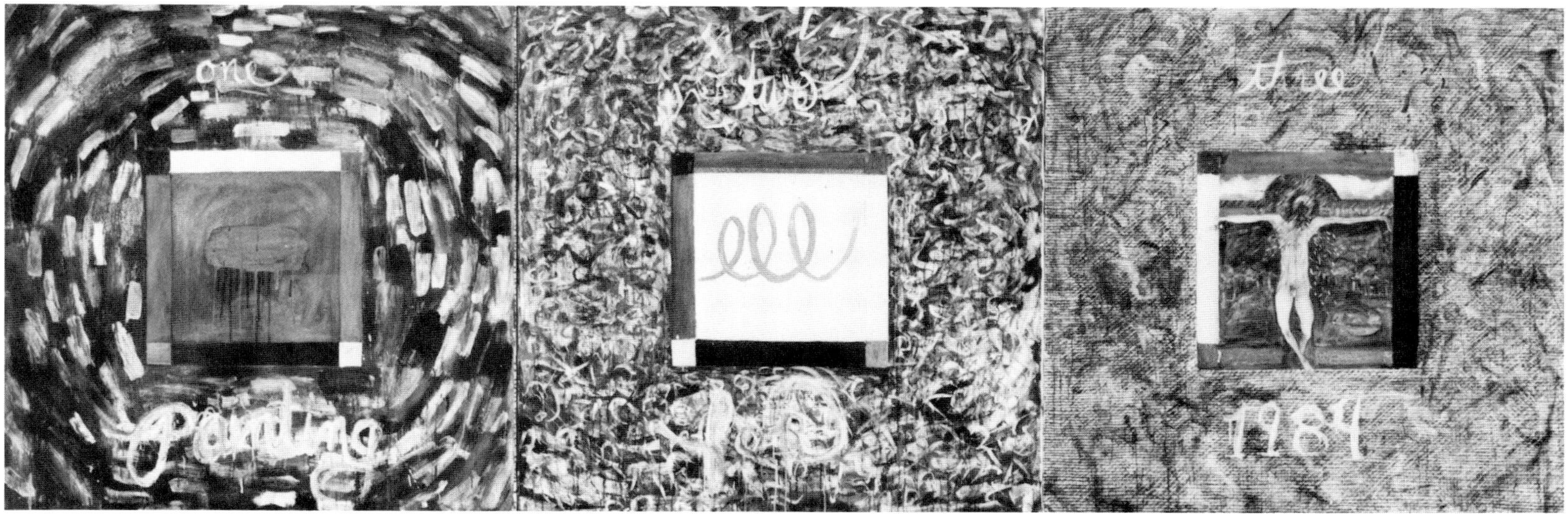

Painting for 1984 1981
Oil on canvas
3 panels, each 42 × 42
Private collection

Icon One: The Mother 1981
Oil on canvas
3 panels, each 48 × 48
Courtesy the artist and Max Protetch Gallery, New York, New York

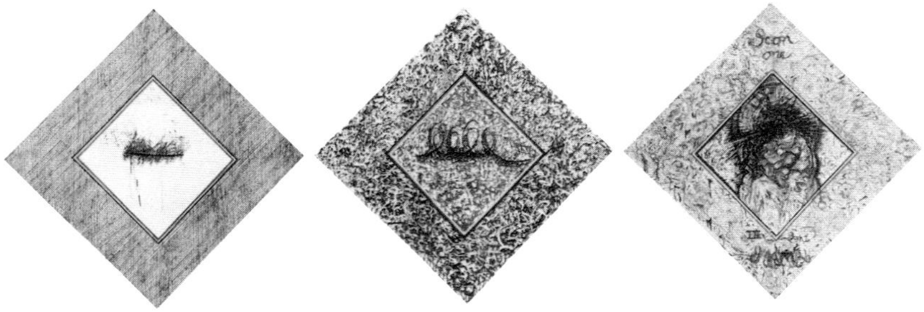

Icon Two: Eros 1981
Oil on canvas
3 panels, each 48 × 48
Courtesy the artist and Max Protetch Gallery, New York, New York

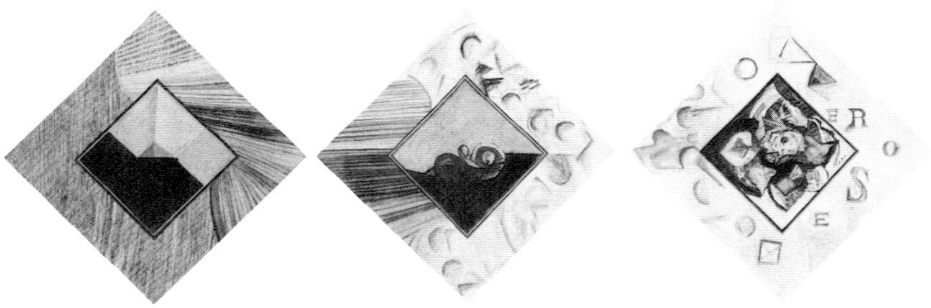

Icon Three: The Boy 1981
Oil on canvas
3 panels, each 48 × 48
Courtesy the artist and Max Protetch Gallery, New York, New York

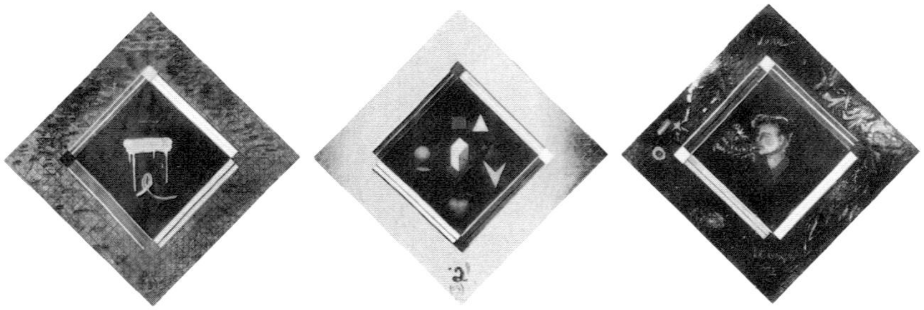

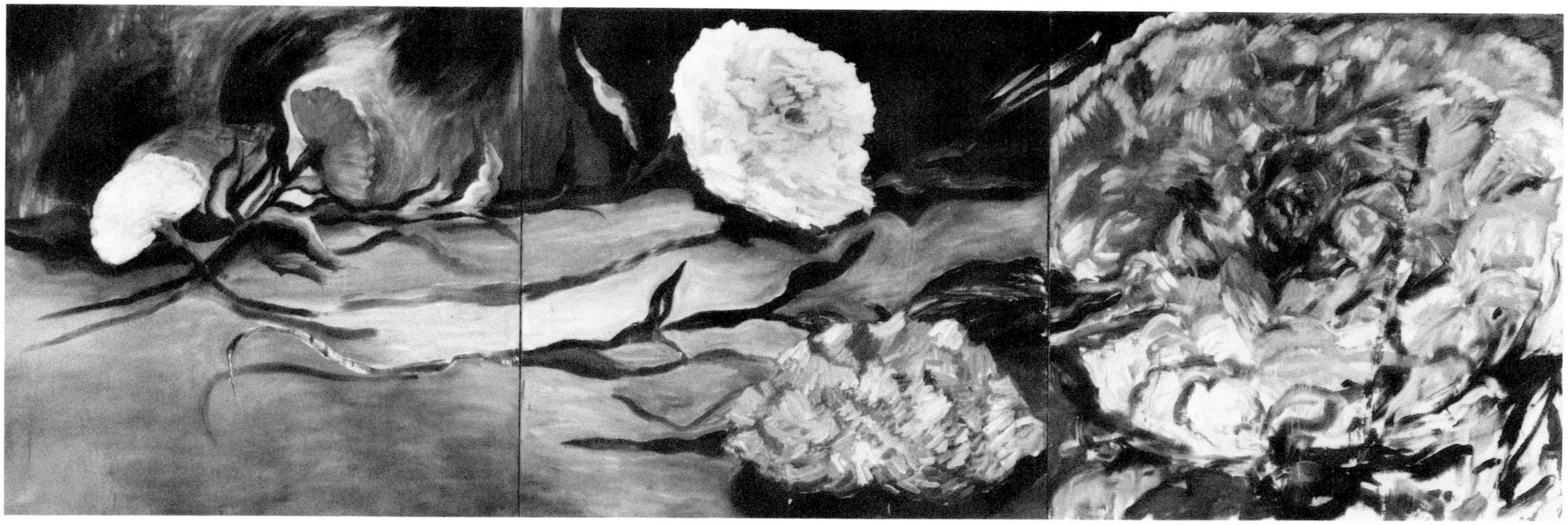

Joost's Carnation Landscape 1981
Oil on canvas
3 panels, each 60 × 60
Sydney and Frances Lewis Collection

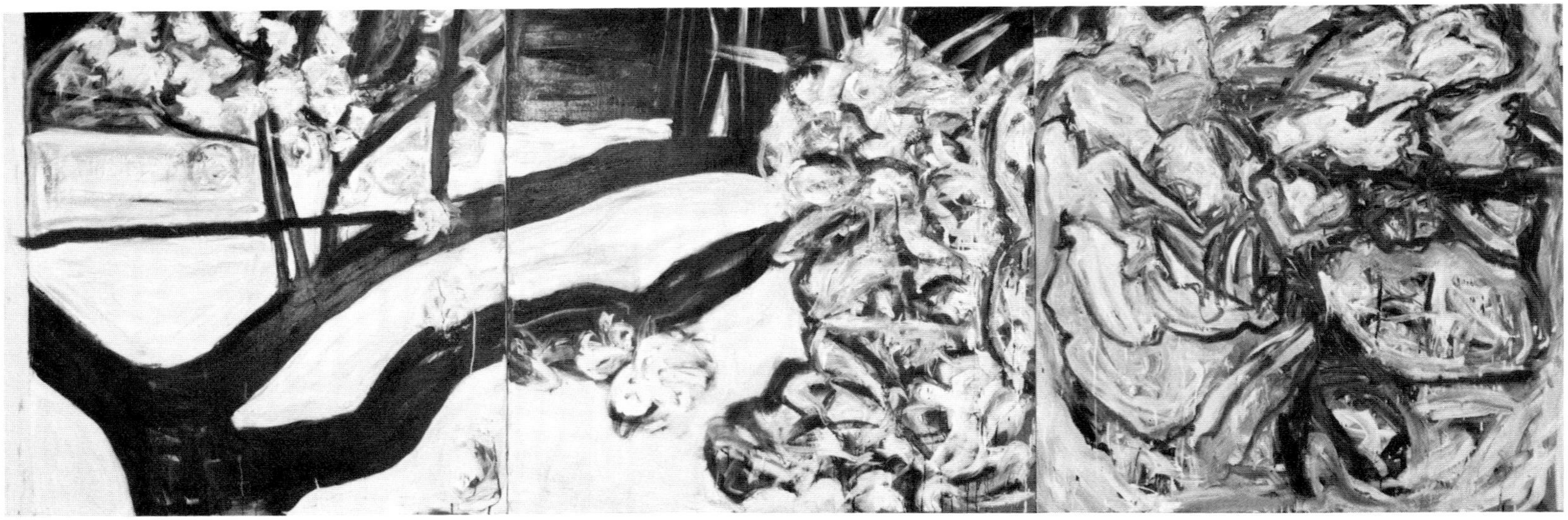

Cherry Blossoms II (In Winter) 1982
Oil on canvas
3 panels, each 60 × 60
McIntosh/Drysdale Gallery, Houston, Texas

Pat Steir

Chronology

1940
Born, Newark, New Jersey.

1956-58
Studied, Pratt Institute, Brooklyn, New York.

1959-60
Studied, Boston Museum School and Boston University, Cambridge, Massachusetts.

1960-62
Studied, Pratt Institute, B.F.A., 1961.

1964
First solo exhibition, Terry Dintenfass Gallery, New York, New York.

1961-64
Begins to do free-lance work in book design and book cover design.

1965-69
Art Director, Harper & Row, New York, New York.

1971
Solo exhibition, Graham Gallery, New York, New York.

1972
Solo exhibitions at both Graham Gallery and Paley & Lowe, Inc., New York, New York. Shows what she considers to be her first mature work. (After this she will show annually in New York except for 1974 and 1979.)

1973
First solo museum exhibition, The Corcoran Gallery of Art, Washington, D.C.

Begins printmaking with Landfall Press, Chicago, Illinois.

1973-75
Lives part of each year in Los Angeles, California, teaching six months at California Institute for the Arts, Valencia; working in New York the remainder of each year.

1974
Awarded Individual Artist's Fellowship, National Endowment for the Arts.

1974-77
Stops painting, continues to draw and make prints. Travels extensively in Europe.

1975
First solo European exhibition, Galerie Farideh Cadot, Paris, France.
Begins printmaking with Crown Point Press, Oakland, California.

1976
Designs, with Sol LeWitt, Lucy Lippard's important book, *Eva Hesse*.

1977
Begins to spend more and more time in Europe, particularly Amsterdam.
Shows extensively in Europe: France, Italy, Sweden, Switzerland.
Founding member, *Printed Matter* and *Heresies*.

1977-82
Continues to show regularly in Europe and America.

1982
Receives the John Simon Guggenheim Memorial Foundation Fellowship.

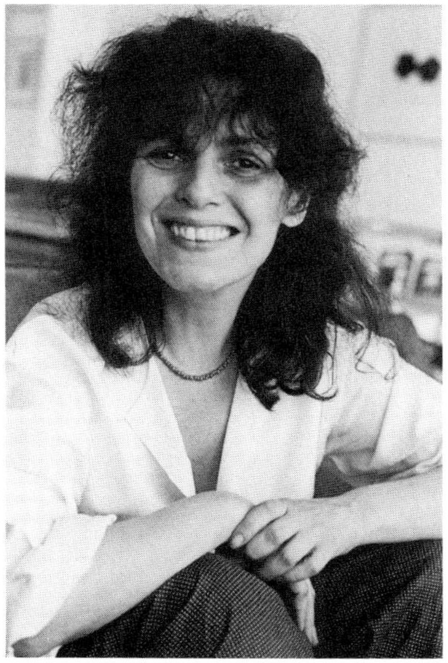

Exhibitions

Solo

1964

Terry Dintenfass Gallery, New York, New York. Oct. 15–Nov. 4.
C[ampbell], L[awrence]. "Pat Steir." *Art News* (New York), v. 63, no. 7, Nov. 1964, p. 22.

1969

Bienville Gallery, New Orleans, Louisiana.

1971

Graham Gallery, New York, New York. *Pat Steir.* Jan. 12–Feb. 16.
Brown, Gordon, "Pat Steir at Graham." *Arts Magazine* (New York), v. 45, no. 4, Feb. 1971, pp. 65-66.
G[ollin], J[ane]. "Pat Steir." *Art News* (New York), v. 69, no. 10, Feb. 1971, p. 26.

1972

Paley & Lowe, Inc., New York, New York. *Pat Steir.* Sep. 30–Oct. 18.
Bordon, Lizzie. "Pat Steir: Paley & Lowe." *Artforum* (New York), v. 11, no. 4, Dec. 1972, p. 88.
Canaday, John. "Art: Two Shows South of Houston St." *The New York Times* (New York), v. 71, Sep. 30, 1972, p. 27.
Crimp, Douglas, "Pat Steir." *Art News* (New York), v. 71, no. 6, Oct. 1972, pp. 82-83.
Matthias, Rosemary. "Pat Steir: Paley & Lowe." *Arts Magazine* (New York), v. 47, no. 2, Nov. 1972, p. 68.
Welish, Marjorie. "New York Letter." *Art International* (Lugano), v. 16, no. 10, Dec. 1972, p. 69.

Douglass College, Rutgers University, New Brunswick, New Jersey. Fall.

1973

Ball State University Art Gallery, Muncie, Indiana. *Pat Steir Drawings.* Feb. 5-28.

The Corcoran Gallery of Art, Washington, D.C. *Pat Steir: Recent Paintings.* Nov. 7–Dec. 9.
Forgey, Benjamin. "3 New Yorkers at Corcoran." *The Washington Star-News* (Washington, D.C.), Nov. 26, 1973, p. C4.
Richard, Paul. "Homage Paid to Nameless Gods." *The Washington Post* (Washington, D.C.), Nov. 13, 1973, p. E7.

Max Protetch Gallery, Washington, D.C. *Pat Steir: Recent Work.*

1975

Fourcade, Droll, Inc., New York, New York. *Pat Steir: Recent Paintings.* Mar. 22–Apr. 19.
Andre, Michael. "Pat Steir." *Art News* (New York), v. 74, no. 6, Summer 1975, p. 144.
Baker, Kenneth. "Pat Steir." *Arts Magazine* (New York), v. 49, no. 8, Apr. 1975, p. 21.
Derfner, Phyllis. "New York." *Art International* (Lugano), v. 19, no. 5, May 1975, p. 66.
Heinemann, Susan. "Pat Steir: Fourcade, Droll, Inc." *Artforum* (New York), v. 13, no. 10, Summer 1975, pp. 75-76.
Russell, John. "Art: In Grosz's Work, a Look at the Hurts of Home." *The New York Times* (New York), v. 74, Apr. 5, 1975, p. 24.

John Doyle Gallery, Paris, France.

State University of New York, Oneonta. (mural)

1976

The Art Gallery, University of Maryland, College Park. *Pat Steir.* Feb. 27–Mar. 28.

Xavier Fourcade, Inc., New York, New York, *Pat Steir: Drawings.* Apr. 20–May 8.
Brach, Paul. "Pat Steir: Xavier Fourcade Gallery." *Artforum* (New York), v. 15, no. 2, Oct. 1976, p. 62.
Crary, Jonathan. "Pat Steir." *Arts Magazine* (New York), v. 50, no. 10, June 1976, p. 10.
Russell, John. "Art: French Neo-Classicism Without The Arguments." *The New York Times* (New York), v. 75, Apr. 24, 1976, p. 19.

Morgan Thomas Gallery, Santa Monica, California. *Pat Steir.* Fall.

Galerie Farideh Cadot, Paris, France. Nov. 16–Dec. 11.

White Gallery, Portland State University, Oregon. *Works by Pat Steir.* Dec. 17, 1976–Jan. 31, 1977.

Otis Art Institute, Los Angeles, California.
Wilson, William. "Downbeat Exhibit at Otis Galleries." *The Los Angeles Times* (Los Angeles), Sep. 6, 1976.

1977

Carl Solway Gallery, Cincinnati, Ohio. *Recent Drawings by Pat Steir.* Apr. 22–May 30.

1978

Droll/Kolbert Gallery, New York, New York. *Pat Steir*. Feb. 28–Mar. 25.
- Cavaliere, Barbara. "Pat Steir." *Arts Magazine* (New York), v. 52, no. 9, May 1978, p. 27.
- McFadden, Sarah. "Pat Steir at Droll/Kolbert." *Art in America* (New York), v. 66, no. 5, Sep./Oct. 1978, p. 118.
- Perrone, Jeff. "Pat Steir at Droll/Kolbert." *Artforum* (New York), v. 16, no. 9, May 1978, pp. 57-58.
- Raynor, Vivien. "Art: Pat Steir, The Expressed Self." *The New York Times* (New York), v. 77, Mar. 10, 1978, p. C23.
- Schwartz, Ellen. "New York Reviews: Pat Steir." *Art News* (New York), v. 77, no. 5, May 1978, p. 186.
- Zimmer, William. "Airing Out the Grid." *The SoHo Weekly News* (New York), Mar. 16, 1978, p. 24.

Galerie Farideh Cadot, Paris, France. *New Paintings*. Mar. 21–Apr. 22.

Galeria Marilena Bonomo, Bari, Italy. *Pat Steir — Early Drawings*. Apr.

Art School for Children, Birmingham, Alabama. (mural)

1979

Galerie Farideh Cadot, Paris, France. Oct. 16–Nov. 24.
- Nuridsany, Michael. "Pat Steir, une puissance magique." *Le Figaro* (Paris), Nov. 16, 1979.

1980

Droll/Kolbert Gallery, New York, New York. *Rembrandt's Hairline*. Feb. 20–Mar. 12.
- Cohen, Ronny H. "Pat Steir, Droll/Kolbert Gallery." *Artforum* (New York), v. 18, no. 9, May 1980, pp. 82-83.
- Glueck, Grace. "Art: Pat Steir." *The New York Times* (New York), v. 79, Feb. 22, 1980, p. C19.

Max Protetch Gallery, New York, New York. *New Paintings*. Mar. 7–Apr. 7.

Galerie d'art contemporain, Geneva, Switzerland. *New Paintings*. Sep. 16–Oct.

Galerie Farideh Cadot, Paris, France *Pat Steir*. Fall.
- Interview with Robin White. "Pat Steir, un expressionnisme réfléchi." *Art Press* (Paris), no. 18, Oct. 1980, p. 17.

1981

Max Protetch Gallery, New York, New York. *Pat Steir: New Work*. Jan. 16–Feb. 7.

Galeria Marilena Bonomo, Bari, Italy. *Pat Steir — Paintings and Wall Drawings*. Feb. 19–Mar.

Galerie Farideh Cadot, Paris, France. *New Paintings*. Mar. 7–Apr. 4.
- Laurent, Rachel. "Pat Steir." *Art Press* (Paris), no. 46, Mar. 1981.

Marianne Deson Gallery, Chicago, Illinois. *Pat Steir*. May 16–Jun. 24.
- Artner, Ellen G. "Art." *Chicago Tribune* (Chicago), Jun. 19, 1981, sec. 2, p. 12.

Bell Gallery, List Art Center, Brown University, Providence, Rhode Island. *Pat Steir*. Sep. 16–Oct. 11.
- Dickinson, Nancy. "Pat Steir: Vital Paintings." *Rhode Island Review Magazine* (Providence), Oct. 1981, p. 12.

Crown Point Press Gallery, Oakland, California. *Pat Steir Etchings and Paintings*. Nov. 14–Dec. 31.
- Levine, Melinda. "Layers, Marks and Hypnotic Regression." *Artweek* (Oakland), v. 12, no. 41, Dec. 5, 1981, pp. 1, 16.
- Shere, Charles. "Steir show opens new Crown Point Gallery." *Oakland Tribune* (Oakland), Dec. 24, 1981, p. C3.

Max Protetch Gallery, New York, New York. *Pat Steir*. Nov. 5–Nov. 28.
- Casademont, Joan. "Pat Steir, Max Protetch Gallery." *Artforum* (New York), v. 20, no. 6, Feb. 1982, p. 84.
- Frank, Elizabeth. "Pat Steir at Max Protetch." *Art in America* (New York), v. 70, no. 3, Mar. 1982, pp. 143-44.
- Phillips, Deborah C. "Pat Steir." *Art News* (New York), v. 81, no. 2, Feb. 1982, pp. 164, 166.
- Russell, John. "Met Unveils Treasures of Islamic Golden Age." *The New York Times* (New York), v. 81, Nov. 20, 1981, p. C28.
- Zimmer, William. "Furniture outlets (or, Formica follows function)." *The SoHo Weekly News* (New York), Dec. 1, 1981, p. 48.

Galleriet, Lund, Sweden. *Pat Steir: Etchings, Lithographs & Drawings*. Nov. 28–Dec. 20.
- Berntsson, Asa. "Konst som liv och manniska." *Sydsvenska Dagbladet* (Malmoe), Dec. 7, 1981.

1982

Eason Gallery, Santa Fe, New Mexico. *Pat Steir: Recent Paintings*. Aug. 3-27.

Nina Freudenheim Gallery, Buffalo, New York. *Pat Steir: New Work*. Sep. 25–Oct. 28.
- Bannon, Anthony. "Steir Uses Sea to Deliver Message." *Buffalo Evening News* (Buffalo), Oct. 7, 1982, p. B13.

Galerie Farideh Cadot, Paris, France. *New Paintings*. Nov. 26–Dec. 23.
Champey, Inès. "Pat Steir." *Art Press* (Paris), no. 67, Feb. 1983.

Galerie Annemarie Verna, Zürich, Switzerland. *Pat Steir*. Dec. 1, 1982–Jan. 8, 1983.
Wechsler, Max (translated from the German by Martha Humphreys). "Zurich: Pat Steir, Galerie Annemarie Verna." *Artforum* (New York), v. 21, no. 8, Apr. 1983, pp. 82-83.

1983
Crown Point Press Gallery, New York, New York. *At Sea, 1982*. (monotypes) Jan. 13–Feb. 19.

Spencer Museum of Art, The University of Kansas, Lawrence. *Form Illusion Myth: Prints and Drawings of Pat Steir*. Jan. 17–Feb. 27. catalogue. Circulated to The University Art Museum, California State University, Long Beach; Contemporary Arts Museum, Houston; The Wellesley College Museum, Jewett Arts Center, Wellesley College, Massachusetts; Brooks Memorial Art Gallery, Memphis, Tennessee.

The Harcus Gallery, Boston, Massachusetts. *Pat Steir: New Paintings*. Mar. 12–Apr. 6.

Fuller Goldeen Gallery, San Francisco, California. *Pat Steir*. Apr. 5-30.

Max Protetch Gallery, New York, New York. *The Tree*. Apr. 8–May 7.

Group

1963
The High Museum of Art, Atlanta, Georgia.

1964

Finch College Museum of Art, New York, New York.

Philadelphia Museum of Art, Pennsylvania. *Annual Exhibition*.

The Museum of Modern Art, New York, New York. *Drawings*.

1966
Terry Dintenfass Gallery, New York, New York.

1969
Graham Gallery, New York, New York.

1970
French and Company, New York, New York.

1971
Glauber Poons Gallery, Amsterdam, the Netherlands.

Graham Gallery, New York, New York.

Paley & Lowe, Inc., New York, New York. *Three Paintings*.

1972
Whitney Museum of American Art, New York, New York. *40th Annual Exhibition*. Jan. 25–Mar. 19. catalogue.

Fine Arts Center, University of Rhode Island, Kingston. *Three Painters*. (Mary Heilmann, Pat Steir, Joan Snyder). Mar. 6-26.

Institute of Contemporary Art, University of Pennsylvania, Philadelphia. *The Topography of Nature: The Microcosm and Macrocosm*. Mar. 22–Apr. 27. catalogue.

Indianapolis Museum of Art, Indiana. *Painting and Sculpture Today, 1972*. Apr. 26–Jun. 4. catalogue.

The Corcoran Gallery of Art, Washington, D.C. *Seven Young Artists: Works on Paper*. (Susan Bienen, Joe Brainard, Alan Bridge, Michael Clark, Ascian, Pat Steir, Jim Sullivan). Aug. 1–Sep. 15.

Aldrich Museum of Contemporary Art, Ridgefield, Connecticut. *Paintings on Paper*. Sep. 17–Dec. 17. catalogue.

Art Lending Service, The Museum of Modern Art, New York, New York. *Landscapes*. Oct. 9–Nov. 15.

Contemporary Arts Center, Cincinnati, Ohio. *Alternative Landscapes*. Oct.

Bard College, Annandale-on-Hudson, New York. *Paintings on Paper*.

1973
Whitney Museum of American Art, New York, New York. *Biennial Exhibition: Contemporary American Art*. Jan. 10–Mar. 18. catalogue.

New York Cultural Center, New York, New York. *Women Choose Women*. Jan. catalogue.

Whitney Museum of American Art, New York, New York. *American Drawings 1963-1973*. May 25-Jun. 22. catalogue.

Institute of Contemporary Art, University of Pennsylvania, Philadelphia. *Six Visions*. Oct. 10–Nov. 25. catalogue.

Cusack Gallery, Houston, Texas. *Drawings*. Dec. 11, 1973–Jan. 8, 1974.

The Museum of Modern Art, New York, New York.

1974

Whitney Museum of American Art, Downtown Branch, New York, New York. *People and Places*. Feb. 27–Apr. 4.

The Civic Center Museum, The Philadelphia Civic Center, Pennsylvania. *Woman's Work: American Art 1974*. Apr. 27–May 26. Cosponsored by the Museum of the Philadelphia Civic Center and organized by FOCUS, Philadelphia Focuses on Women in the Visual Arts. catalogue.

Indianapolis Museum of Art, Indiana. *Painting and Sculpture Today, 1974*. May 22–Jul. 14. catalogue. Circulated to Contemporary Arts Center, Cincinnati, Ohio.

Institute of Contemporary Art, Boston, Massachusetts. *Joan Snyder and Pat Steir*. Oct. 1–Nov. 12. catalogue.

Baker, Kenneth. "Joan Snyder and Pat Steir at the ICA." *Art in America* (New York), v. 63, no. 2, Mar./Apr. 1975, pp. 105, 107.

Heinemann, Susan. "Pat Steir, Joan Snyder, Institute of Contemporary Art, Boston." *Artforum* (New York), v. 13, no. 4, Dec. 1974, p. 75.

Taylor, Robert. "Joan Snyder and Pat Steir: The Outer World and the 'Inner' Self." *Boston Sunday Globe* (Boston), Oct. 6, 1974, p. 81.

Loretta Yarlow Fine Arts, Ltd., Toronto, Canada. *Inaugural Exhibition*.

The Saidye Bronfman Centre, Montreal, Canada. *28 Painters of the New York Avant-Garde '74*.

1975

The American Federation of Arts, New York, New York. *Recent Drawings*. (William Allan, James Bishop, Vija Celmins, Brice Marden, Jim Nutt, Alan Saret, Pat Steir, Richard Tuttle) Jun. 15, 1975–Oct. 10, 1976. catalogue. Circulated to Huntsville Museum of Art, University of Alabama, Von Braun Civic Center, Huntsville, Alabama; The Art Museum, Princeton University, New Jersey; The Cummer Gallery of Art, Jacksonville, Florida; State University of New York, Stony Brook.

Fourcade, Droll, Inc., New York, New York. *Group Show*. (Michael Heizer, Joan Mitchell, Joseph Cornell, Willem de Kooning, Pat Steir). Jun. –Jul. 31.

Ellenzweig, Allen. "Group Show." *Arts Magazine* (New York), v. 50, no. 2, Oct. 75, p. 13.

Whitney Museum of American Art, Downtown Branch, New York, New York. *25 Stills*. Oct. 30–Dec. 3.

Gallery 210, University of Missouri, St. Louis. *American Women Printmakers*. Oct. catalogue. Circulated to Cottey College, Nevada, Missouri; Southeast Missouri State University, Cape Girardeau; Northeast Missouri State University Gallery, Maryville; Prudential Savings and Loan, Union, Missouri; Forest Park Community College, St. Louis, Missouri; Jefferson College, Hillsboro, Missouri; University of Missouri, Kansas City; Missouri Western College, St. Joseph.

Max Protetch Gallery, Washington, D.C. *Art That Involves Words*.

1976

Marion Koogler McNay Art Institute, San Antonio, Texas. *American Artists '76: A Celebration*. May 23–Aug. 1. catalogue.

Indianapolis Museum of Art, Indiana. *Painting and Sculpture Today 1976*. Jun. 9–Jul. 18. catalogue.

The University Art Museum, California State University, Long Beach. *16 Projects/4 Artists*. Sep. 12, 1976–Mar. 25, 1977. catalogue. Circulated to Wright State University Art Gallery, Dayton, Ohio; Moore College of Art Gallery, Philadelphia, Pennsylvania; University of Kentucky Art Gallery, Lexington.

Philadelphia College of Art Gallery, Pennsylvania. *Private Notations: Artists's Sketchbooks II*. Oct. 23–Nov. 24. catalogue.

Max Protetch Gallery, Washington, D.C.

1977

Whitney Museum of American Art, New York, New York. *1977 Biennial*. Feb. 15–Apr. 3. catalogue.

Forgey, Benjamin. "The Whitney Biennial." *Art News* (New York), v. 76, no. 4, Apr. 1977, pp. 120-21.

Glueck, Grace. "Art People." *The New York Times* (New York), v. 76, Jan. 14, 1977, p. C16.

Art Institute of Chicago, Illinois. *Drawings of the 70s*. Mar. 12–May 1. catalogue.

P.S. 1, Institute for Art and Urban Resources, Long Island City, New York. *A Painting Show*. May 1-29.

New York State Women's Meeting, Albany, New York. *Women in Art: Working Papers*. Summer.

Archer M. Huntington Gallery, University Art Museum, The University of Texas at Austin. *New in the Seventies*. Aug. 21–Sep. 25. catalogue.

San Diego Museum of Art, California. *Invitational American Drawing Exhibition*. Sep. 17–Oct. 30. catalogue.

The Museum of Modern Art, New York, New York. *America Drawn and Matched.* Sep. 20–Dec. 4.

Nelson Gallery of Art, Atkins Museum of Fine Arts, Kansas City, Missouri. *New Prints Acquisitions.* Fall.

Weatherspoon Art Gallery, University of North Carolina at Greensboro. *Art on Paper, 1977.* Nov. 13–Dec. 18. catalogue.

Museum of Contemporary Art, Chicago, Illinois. *A Survey of Prints (1970-1977).* Nov. 18, 1977–Jan. 8, 1978. catalogue.

Madison Art Center, Wisconsin. *Recent Works on Paper by American Artists.* Dec. 4, 1977–Jan. 15, 1978. catalogue.

1978

University Art Museum, University of California, Santa Barbara. *Contemporary Drawing/New York.* Feb. 22–Mar. 26. catalogue.

Touchstone Gallery, New York, New York. *Beyond the Canvas . . . Artists' Books and Notations.* Nov. 4–30.
Buonagurio, Edgar. "Artists' Books and Notations." *Arts Magazine* (New York), v. 53, no. 3, Nov. 1978, p. 5.
Lubell, Ellen. "Interrupted Thoughts." *The SoHo Weekly News* (New York), Nov. 30, 1978, pp. 28, 47.
Rickey, Carrie. "Beyond the Canvas . . . Artists' Books and Notations." *Artforum* (New York), v. 17, no. 6, Feb. 1979, pp. 60-61.

Janus Gallery, Los Angeles, California. *Drawing Explorations 1930-1978.* Nov. 17–Dec. 23.
Singerman, Howard. "Interpretations of the Role of Drawing." *Artweek* (Oakland), v. 9, no. 42, Dec. 9, 1978, p. 6.

Albright-Knox Art Gallery, Buffalo, New York. *American Painting of the 1970s.* Dec. 8, 1978–Jan. 14, 1979. catalogue. Circulated to Newport Harbor Art Museum, Newport Beach, California; The Oakland Museum, California; Cincinnati Art Museum, Ohio; Art Museum of South Texas, Corpus Christi; Krannert Art Museum, University of Illinois, Champaign.

1979

The New Museum, New York, New York. *The 1970's New American Painting.* Jun. 15, 1979–Feb. 15, 1981. catalogue. Exhibition organized by The New Museum and sponsored by the International Communications Agency, Washington, D.C. Opened at the National Museum, Belgrade, Yugoslavia and circulated to the National Museum, Zagreb, Yugoslavia; Modern Galerija, Ljubljana, Yugoslavia; Fiera Della Saidengna, Cagliari, Sardinia; Civica Galleria d'Arte Moderna, Palermo, Sicily; North Jutland Museum, Copenhagen, Denmark; Nepliget Park, Budapest, Hungary; Parcul Herastran, Bucharest, Hungary; BWA Gallery, Torun, Poland; Ministry of Culture, Lodes, Poland; National Museum, Warsaw, Poland.

Whitney Museum of American Art, New York, New York. *Decade in Review: Selections from the 1970s Permanent Collection.* Jun. 19–Sep. 3.

Art Museum, The University of New Mexico, Albuquerque. *Lithography: A Sense of Scale.* Sep. 30–Nov. 4.

Union Carbide Building, Inner City Scholarship Fund, New York, New York. *Art from Corporate Collections.*

1980

Nina Freudenheim Gallery, Buffalo, New York. *Drawings.* Jan. 12–Feb. 7.
Huntington, Richard. "'Drawings' Exhibit at Freudenheim." *Buffalo Courier-Express* (Buffalo), Jan. 20, 1980, p. F4.
"Show Promotes Raised Status of Drawings." *Buffalo Evening News* (Buffalo), Jan. 26, 1980, p. A8.

Whitney Museum of American Art, New York, New York. *American Painting of the 60s and 70s The Real, The Ideal, The Fantastic: Selections from the Whitney Museum of American Art.* Apr. 3, 1980–May 25, 1981. Circulated.

The Brooklyn Museum, New York, New York. *American Drawings in Black & White: 1970-1980.* Nov. 22, 1980–Jan. 18, 1981. catalogue.

Walker Art Center, Minneapolis, Minnesota. *Artist and Printer Six American Print Studios.* Dec. 7, 1980–Jan. 18, 1981. catalogue.

Max Protetch Gallery, New York, New York.
Phillips, Deborah C. "Reviews." *Arts Magazine* (New York), v. 55, no. 8, Apr. 1981, p. 29.

1981

Nina Freudenheim Gallery, Buffalo, New York. *Paper Work.* Mar. 7–Apr. 1.
Foran, Jack. "Fine Show of Works on Paper in the Nina Freudenheim Gallery." *The Buffalo Evening News* (Buffalo), Mar. 13, 1981, Gusto section, p. 35.
Huntington, Richard. "Tough, Peaceful 'Paper Work' Show." *Buffalo Courier-Express* (Buffalo), Mar. 15, 1981, pp. E1, E6.

The Patrick Gallery, Austin, Texas. *Rigors.* May 12–Jun. 13.

Cittá di Noto, Siracusa, Italy. *Aljofre Barroco.* May 24–Jun. 31. catalogue.
Paparoni, Demetrio. "Irregolare è bello." *La Sicilia,* date unknown, p. 3.

Clark-Benton Gallery, Santa Fe, New Mexico. *New York News.* Jun. 12–Jul. 1.

Sordoni Art Gallery, Wilkes College, Wilkes-Barre, Pennsylvania. *A Range of Contemporary Drawings.* Aug. 31–Sep. 20.

Art Lending Service, The Museum of Modern Art, New York, New York. *A Penthouse Aviary*. Sep. 24, 1981–Jan. 7, 1982.

Wesleyan University Art Gallery and the Davison Art Center, Wesleyan University, Middletown, Connecticut. (in association with the Wadsworth Atheneum, Hartford, Connecticut.) *No Title: The Collection of Sol LeWitt*. Oct. 21–Dec. 20. catalogue.

Weatherspoon Art Gallery, University of North Carolina at Greensboro. *Art on Paper, 1981*. Nov. 15–Dec. 13. catalogue.

Gloria Luria Gallery, Bay Harbor Islands, Florida. *Pat Steir — Denise Green*. Dec. 11, 1981–Jan. 9, 1982.

Jacksonville Art Museum, Florida. *Currents: A New Mannerism*. Dec. 11, 1981–Jan. 24, 1982. catalogue. Circulated to the University of South Florida Art Galleries, Tampa.

1982

Mulvane Art Center, Washburn University, Topeka, Kansas. *Shea Gordon, Pat Steir and Denise Green*. Mar. 7-28.
Navone, Edward. "Art and Words." *Forum* (Kansas City, Missouri), Apr. 1982, p. 10-11.

Madison Art Center, Wisconsin. *New American Graphics 2*. Mar. 13–Apr. 25.

Fuller Goldeen Gallery, San Francisco, California. *Paintings*. Mar. 31–Apr. 24.

DuBose Galleries, Houston, Texas. *Flowers and Gardens in American Painting*. May 2–Jun. 4.

Crown Point Press Gallery, Oakland, California. *Representing Reality: Fragments from the Image Field An Exhibition of Etchings and Woodblock Prints by Günter Brus, Francesco Clemente, Joel Fisher, Robert Kushner, Pat Steir, William T. Wiley*. Aug./Sep. catalogue. Circulated to University Art Collections, Arizona State University, Tempe; Contemporary Arts Center, Cincinnati, Ohio; Huntsville Museum of Art, Alabama; University Art Gallery, New Mexico State University, Las Cruces; Art Museum, The University of New Mexico, Albuquerque.

John C. Stoller & Company, Minneapolis, Minnesota. *New American Painting III*. (Lynda Benglis, Pat Steir, Robert Zakanitch). Sep. 17–Dec. 10.

Aldrich Museum of Contemporary Art, Ridgefield, Connecticut. *Post-Minimalisms*. Sep. 19, 1982–Jan. 2, 1983.

Vassar College Art Gallery, Poughkeepsie, New York. *Geometric Art at Vassar*. Nov. 1, 1982–Feb. 6, 1983.

Musée d'art contemporain, Paris, France. *L'art Baroque*.

1983

Gallerie Annemarie Verna, Zürich, Switzerland. *When Art Becomes Book When Books Become Art*. Feb. 5–Mar. 22.

The Port of History Museum at Penn's Landing, Philadelphia, Pennsylvania. *Printed by Women: A National Exhibition of Photographs and Prints*. Feb. 17–Mar. 27.

A Space, Toronto, Canada. *Sex and Representation*. Feb. 28–Mar. 19.
Mays, John Bentley. "Steering Clear of Painterly Hot Sauce." *The Globe and Mail* (Toronto), Mar. 11, 1983, p. E5.

Whitney Museum of American Art, New York, New York. *1983 Biennial Exhibition*. Mar. 15–May 22. catalogue.

Centre culturel le Parvi, Tarbes, France. Group Exhibition. Apr. 22–May 31.

Barbara Mathes Gallery, New York, New York. *Inaugural Exhibition*. Apr. 23–May 28.

Impressions Gallery, Boston, Massachusetts. *Tulip Time*. May 5-31.

Musée d'art de Toulons, France. *Recent Acquisitions*.

Musée d'art moderne de la ville de Paris, France. *ARC Exhibition*.

Bibliography

Albright-Knox Art Gallery, Buffalo, New York. *American Painting of the 1970s.* Dec. 8, 1978–Jan. 14, 1979. Foreword by Robert T. Buck, Jr. Acknowledgments and essay by Linda L. Cathcart.

Aldrich Museum of Contemporary Art, Ridgefield, Connecticut. *Exhibitions Fall 1972: Selections from the Aldrich Museum Collection and the Invitational Showing of "Paintings on Paper."* Sep. 17–Dec. 17, 1972. Introduction by Larry Aldrich.

The American Federation of Arts, New York, New York. *Recent Drawings.* Jun. 15, 1975–Oct. 10, 1976. Introduction and essay by Elke M. Solomon.

Andre, Michael. "Pat Steir." *Art News* (New York), v. 75, no. 7, Sep. 1976, pp. 68-69.

Art Institute of Chicago, Illinois. *Drawings of the 70s.* Mar. 9–May 1, 1977. Introduction by Harry Joachim.

Baker, Kenneth. "The World Within Around Us." *Christian Science Monitor* (Boston), Nov. 17, 1972.

Bell Gallery, List Art Center, Brown University, Providence, Rhode Island. *Pat Steir.* Sep. 16–Oct. 11, 1981. Statement by Pat Steir.

Boorsch, Suzanne. "New Editions: Pat Steir." *Art News* (New York), v. 77, no. 3, Mar. 1978, p. 137.

The Brooklyn Museum, New York. *American Drawings in Black & White: 1970–1980.* Nov. 22, 1980–Jan. 18, 1981. Essay by Gene Baro.

Castle, Ted. "Pat Steir and the Science of the Admirable." *Artforum* (New York), v. 20, no. 9, May 1982, pp. 47-55.

Cittá di noto, Siracusa, Italy. *Aljofre Barroco.* May 25–Jun. 31, 1981. Introduction by Ernesto Rizza and Antonio Vella. Statement by Demetrio Paparoni.

Crown Point Press, Oakland, California. *Pat Steir Etchings and Paintings.* Nov. 14–Dec. 31, 1981. Pat Steir in conversation with Kathan Brown.

Crown Point Press, Oakland, California. *Representing Reality: Fragments from the Image Field An Exhibition of Etchings and Woodblock Prints by Günter Brus, Francesco Clemente, Joel Fisher, Robert Kushner, Pat Steir, William T. Wiley.* Aug./Sep. 1982. Essay by Kathan Brown.

Day, Holliday T. "Midwest Art, A Special Report: Indianapolis, Cincinnati, Dayton." *Art in America* (New York), v. 67, no. 4, Jul./Aug. 1979, pp. 68-71.

Glueck, Grace. "Artists' Conference Alights at a South Seas Island." *The New York Times* (New York), Feb. 24, 1980, p. 44.

Henry, Gerrit. "Is New York still the artistic place to be?" *Art News* (New York), v. 75, no. 9, Nov. 1976, pp. 42-47.

Horsfield, Kate and Blumenthal, Lyn. "Pat Steir." *Profile* (Art Institute of Chicago, Illinois), v. 1, no. 6, Nov. 1981.

Hughes, Robert. "Myths of 'Sensibility'." *Time* (New York) Mar. 20, 1972, pp. 72-77.

Archer M. Huntington Gallery, University Art Museum, The University of Texas at Austin. *New in the Seventies.* Aug. 21–Sep. 25, 1977. Statements by Donald B. Goodall and Fred Seabolt.

Indianapolis Museum of Art, Indiana. *Painting and Sculpture Today, 1972.* Apr. 26–Jun. 4, 1972.

Indianapolis Museum of Art, Indiana. *Painting and Sculpture Today, 1974.* May 22–Jul. 14, 1974. Preface by Carla Weinhardt. Introduction by Richard Warrum.

Indianapolis Museum of Art, Indiana. *Painting and Sculpture Today, 1976.* Jun. 9–Jul. 18, 1976.

Institute of Contemporary Art, Boston, Massachusetts. *Joan Snyder and Pat Steir.* Oct. 1–Nov. 12, 1974. Acknowledgment by Gabriella Jeppson. Essay by Kenneth Baker.

Institute of Contemporary Art, University of Pennsylvania, Philadelphia. *Six Visions.* Oct. 10–Nov. 25, 1973. Acknowledgments and introduction by Suzanne Delehanty.

Institute of Contemporary Art, University of Pennsylvania, Philadelphia. *The Topography of Nature: The Microcosm and Macrocosm.* Mar. 22–Apr. 27, 1972.

International Communications Agency, Washington, D.C. *The 1970's: New American Painting.* Jun. 15, 1979–Feb. 15, 1981. Acknowledgment by Marcia Tucker. Essay by Alan Schwartzman and Kathleen Thomas. Printed in Serbo-Croatian *Az 1970–es évek' uj amerikai festészete.*

Jacksonville Museum of Art, Florida and the University of South Florida, Tampa. *Currents: A New Mannerism.* Dec. 11, 1981–Jan. 24, 1982. Essay by Margaret Miller.

Lyons, Harriet. "Pat Steir: Interior Landscapes." *MS. Magazine* (New York), v. 4, no. 9, Mar. 1976, pp. 34, 36-37.

Madison Art Center, Wisconsin. *Recent Works on Paper by American Artists.* Dec. 7, 1977–Jan. 15, 1978. Introduction by Victor Kord. Statement by Joseph Wilfer.

Marion Koogler McNay Art Institute, San Antonio, Texas. *American Artists '76: A Celebration.* May 23–Aug. 1, 1976. Foreword by John P. Leeper. Essay by Alice C. Simkins.

Museum of Contemporary Art, Chicago, Illinois. *A Survey of Prints (1970–1977)*. Nov. 18, 1977–Jan. 8, 1978. Introduction by Judith Russi Kirshner. Interview of Jack Lemon by Pauline Saliga.

New York Cultural Center, New York. *Women Choose Women*. Jan. 1973. Essay by Lucy R. Lippard.

Perreault, John. "Report from Micronesia: Panoply on Ponape." *Art in America* (New York), v. 68, no. 5, May 1980, pp. 35-39.

Philadelphia College of Art Gallery, Pennsylvania. *Private Notations: Artists's Sketchbooks II*. Oct. 23–Nov. 24, 1976. Essay by Janet Kardon. Statements by the artists.

San Diego Museum of Art, California. *Invitational American Drawing Exhibition*. Sep. 17-Oct. 30, 1977. Acknowledgments by Henry G. Gardiner. Introduction by G. A. Santangelo.

Silverthorne, Jeanne. "The Pressure to Paint." *Artforum* (New York), v. 21, no. 2, Oct. 1982, pp. 67-68.

Simon, Joan. "Expressionism Today: An Artists' Symposium." *Art in America* (New York), v. 70, no. 11, Dec. 1982, pp. 74-75.

Spencer Museum of Art, The University of Kansas, Lawrence. *Form Illusion Myth: Prints and Drawings of Pat Steir*. Jan. 17–Feb. 27, 1983. Acknowledgments, introduction and essay by Elizabeth Broun. Essay by Joan Simon. Interview with and fable by Pat Steir.

Tucker, Marcia. "Interview with Pat Steir." *Journal of the Los Angeles Institute of Contemporary Art* (Los Angeles), no. 10, Mar./Apr. 1976, pp. 22-25.

Tucker, Marcia. "The thing itself, made by me." *Art in America* (New York), v. 61, no. 1, Jan./Feb. 1973, pp. 70-74.

The University Art Museum, California State University, Long Beach. *16 Projects/4 Artists*. Sep. 12, 1976–Mar. 25, 1977. Essays by Lawrence Alloway, Kevin Boyle, Stacy Dukes, William Scurlock and Diane Vanderlip.

University Art Museum, University of California, Santa Barbara. *Contemporary Drawing/New York*. Feb. 22–Mar. 26, 1978. Acknowledgment, foreword and essay by Phyllis Plous.

University of Missouri, St. Louis. *American Women Printmakers*. Oct. 1975. Essay by Sylvia Solochek Walters.

Walker Art Center, Minneapolis, Minnesota. *Artist and Printer Six American Print Studios*. Dec. 7, 1980–Jan. 18, 1981.

Weatherspoon Art Gallery, University of North Carolina, Greensboro. *Art on Paper, 1977*. Nov. 13–Dec. 18, 1977.

Weatherspoon Art Gallery, University of North Carolina, Greensboro. *Art on Paper, 1981*. Nov. 15–Dec. 13, 1981. Foreword by Scott C. Keener.

Wesleyan University Art Gallery and Davison Art Center, Wesleyan University, Middletown, Connecticut. *No Title: The Collection of Sol LeWitt*. Oct. 21–Dec. 20, 1981. Statement by Sol LeWitt. Preface and introduction by John T. Paoletti. Statement by Andrea Miller-Keller and Tracy Atkinson. Commentaries on the artists.

White, Robin. *View* (Crown Point Publications, Oakland), v. 1, no. 3, June 1978, pp. 1-16. Interview with Pat Steir at Crown Point Press.

Whitney Museum of American Art, New York, New York. *40th Annual Exhibition*. Jan. 25–Mar. 19, 1972.

Whitney Museum of American Art, New York, New York. *Biennial Exhibition: Contemporary American Art*. Jan. 10–Mar. 18, 1973. Foreword by John I. H. Baur.

Whitney Museum of American Art, New York, New York. *American Drawing 1963–1973*. May 25–Jun. 22, 1973. Essay by Elke Solomon.

Whitney Museum of American Art, New York, New York. *1977 Biennial*. Feb. 15–Apr. 3, 1977. Foreword by Tom Armstrong. Introduction by Barbara Haskell, Marcia Tucker and Patterson Sims.

Whitney Museum of American Art, New York, New York. *1983 Biennial Exhibition*. Mar. 15–May 22, 1983. Foreword by Tom Armstrong. Preface by John G. Hanhardt, Barbara Haskell, Richard Marshall and Patterson Sims.

Staff

Linda L. Cathcart, Director
Marti Mayo, Curator
Vicki Bailey, Secretary to Membership Officer
Michael J. Barry, Head Preparator
Emily Croll, Registrar
Janet Foreman, Bookkeeper
Sally Gall, Coordinator of Special Projects
Clay Henley, Assistant Preparator
Lynn Hurst, Receptionist/Secretary to the Curator
Rosemary Mackin, Secretary to the Development Officer
Martha R. Prozeller, Membership Officer
Pamela A. Riddle, Development Officer
Sheila Rosenstein, Coordinator, Members' Sales and Rental Gallery
Alexa Stathacos, The Museum Shop Manager
Emily L. Todd, Curatorial Assistant
Ernest Vaughn, Head Security Officer
Timothy Walters, Publications and Public Relations Officer

Photography Credits
Bevan Davies, New York, New York, pp. 33, 34, 35, 36, 37, 38.
Marianne Deson Gallery, Chicago, Illinois, p. 30.
D. James Dee, New York, New York, cover and pp. 44, 45, 31.
Leslie Harris, New York, New York, pp. 29, 32, 41, 43, 46.
Bruce C. Jones, New York, New York, p. 39, left.
Max Protetch Gallery, New York, New York, pp. 40, 42.
Tom Van Enyde, Chicago, Illinois, p. 28.

Board of Trustees

Design by **Creel Morrell Inc**, Houston, Texas
1500 copies printed by **Printmasters Inc**, Austin, Texas
Typesetting by **Encom Graphics**, Houston, Texas